Weekend Walks

in Historic New England

Weekend Walks

in Historic New England

45 Self-Guided Walking Tours
in Cities, Towns, and Villages

Robert J. Regalbuto

BACK COUNTRY

Backcountry Guides
Woodstock, Vermont

Library of Congress Cataloging-in-Publication Data:

Data has been applied for.

Cover design by Dede Cummings Designs
Interior design by Chelsea Cloeter
Maps by Moore Creative Designs © 2003 The Countryman Press
Cover photo of Lexington Common, Lexington, Massachusetts
© Kindra Clineff

Published by Backcountry Guides, an imprint of
The Countryman Press, P.O. Box 748,
Woodstock, Vermont 05091

Distributed by W.W. Norton & Company, Inc.,
500 Fifth Avenue, New York, NY 10110

Printed in the United States of America

10 9 8 7 6 5 4 3 2 1

To John Hinman, M.D.

The object of walking is to relax the mind. . . .
[W]hile you walk . . . divert yourself by the objects surrounding you.

Walking is the best possible exercise.

Habituate yourself to walk very far.

—*Thomas Jefferson, 1785*

Contents

III. Rhode Island

IV. Connecticut

V. New Hampshire

VI. Vermont

VII. Maine

Acknowledgments

Traveling through New England to research this book was a pleasure, not only for the sights seen, but also for the many I have met along the way who generously shared their time and knowledge. Without their information and cooperation this guide could not have been completed, and I am very grateful.

I would be remiss not to say a word of thanks to my colleagues at the Preservation Society of Newport County for their interest and encouragement, especially Joann Blumsack for her many suggestions for the book's contents, and Bill Murphy for his technical support on the word processor.

I am particularly grateful to Deborah Grahame for her sound advice and direction, and to Kermit Hummel, Editorial Director of Countryman Press, for all that he has done to make this work possible.

No acknowledgment would be complete without a special word of gratitude to John Hinman, M.D. I am indebted to him for his advice and commentary on nearly every aspect of the book, and for his generosity, giving many hours of his retirement time to read and offer editorial comment on the manuscript.

Introduction

"Walking is the best exercise. Habituate yourself to walk very far," wrote Thomas Jefferson. This book takes Jefferson's advice a step farther. Beyond walking as exercise, this has been written as your guide to significant sites as you walk along New England's cobbled byways and country roads.

This guide has been written for a broad spectrum of readers—families and other folks, young and old—who have an interest in exploring New England in depth, at eye level, and up close, and at their own pace while at the same time benefitting from a healthy walk.

Weekend Walks in Historic New England contains forty-five distinctive, self-guided walking tours through New England's most historic and picturesque neighborhoods, towns, and villages. Most walks in this guide are about two miles long and are doable in a half day. Of course, each walk may be abbreviated or expanded according to the walker's pace and interests. Each chapter has directions to the walk (by car and by public transportation), an introductory overview, route directions with an accompanying map, and vignettes about places of interest you'll see. The walking tours feature many museums and historic sites, most of which charge admission. As fees and schedules change frequently, telephone numbers and web addresses accompany the site listings so that you may access current information in planning your walk.

Whether you choose to walk in Boston or well beyond its city limits, in mill towns or more remote "picture postcard" villages, along rocky shores or surrounded by rolling hills, this book will lead you on the best walking route and to the most worthwhile destinations in each locale. Enjoy your walking tours, and enjoy all New England has to offer!

I. Massachusetts: Boston and Cambridge

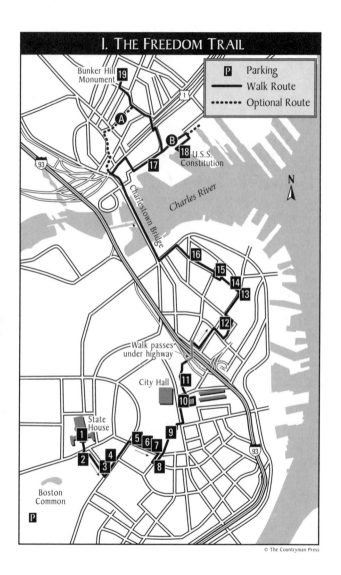

1 • The Freedom Trail

Directions: *By car:* Park at or near the Boston
Common Garage. Call 617-954-2096 for
directions to the garage from all points.
By public transportation: Take the T Red or
Green Line to Park Street (1-800-392-6100,
www.mbta.com).

The Freedom Trail links 16 historic sites in Boston,
all accessible by foot and walkable in a day. It is,
without a doubt, the best known, most popular, and
most trodden historic walking tour in America. While
the sites have been here since colonial times, putting
them together in a walking tour was the idea of William
Schofiled, a Boston journalist, in 1958.

The path of the Freedom Trail is clearly marked with
a red line. Take this book with you; it will describe every
stop on the Freedom Trail and in many cases supply
additional information about other sites along the way.

The trail begins atop Beacon Hill at the Massachusetts State House (1). Before entering the State House
gate turn around and look at Boston Common. The
acreage was set aside for public or "common" use in
1640. Through the centuries it has been used for recre-
ation, walks, public gatherings (both celebrations and
demonstrations), grazing sheep, training and encamp-
ing the military, duels, executions, and burials.

Across from the State House, at the entrance to the Common, note the Robert Gould Shaw Memorial (2). In this bas relief artist Augustus Saint-Gaudens captured the moment in 1863 when Colonel Shaw and the 54th Massachusetts Regiment marched past the State House en route to fight to save the Union. The 54th was the first company made up of free black men who volunteered to fight for the Union. The story of the 54th Massachusetts Regiment was retold in the 1989 film *Glory*, which starred Matthew Broderick as Col. Shaw with Denzel Washington and Morgan Freeman.

Now turn your attention to the State House. Supreme Court Justice Oliver Wendell Holmes said "Boston State-house is the hub of the solar system." The central, red brick section of the house and its gilded dome and cupola (1795) are the work of Charles Bulfinch, a Boston native. On the advice of Thomas Jefferson he toured Europe after graduating from Harvard and studied classical architecture in Italy and France, and the work of Robert Adam in Britain. The granite wings flanking Bulfinch's work were added in 1914. An earlier, yellow brick wing had been added to the rear in 1895.

Before entering the State House look at the statues on the capitol grounds. These memorialize Henry Cabot Lodge (senator), Anne Hutchinson (pioneer advocate for religous tolerance), Horace Mann (educator), Daniel Webster (statesman), Gen. Joseph Hooker, and Mary Dyer, who was hanged on the Common in 1660, because she was a Quaker.

Visit the interior of the State House. Guided tours are available (617-727-3676, www.mass.gov.mass.statehouse). On entering you'll be in Bulfinch's Doric Hall which in turn leads to the Hall of Flags and the Marble

Senate Staircase Hall. Once you've ascended the staircase you'll see the Governor's Office, Senate Reception Room, Senate Chamber, and the House Chamber where the Sacred Cod hangs—long a symbol of the Bay State and once a staple food. Complete your visit at the Archive Museum in the basement.

Walk down Park Street to the Park Street Church (3). Built on the site of the Old Granary, this Congregational Church was built in 1809. Note the elegant classical revival spire and the unusual semicircular porch. The abolitionist Henry Ward Beecher orated fiery sermons here at "Brimstone Corner." William Lloyd Garrison preached his first antislavery sermon here.

The next stop is the Old Granary Burial Ground (4), entered through granite gateposts bearing inverted torches, symbols of death. The gate list the names of the notable persons buried here, among them John Hancock, Samuel Adams, Paul Revere, Benjamin Franklin's parents, and the victims of the Boston Massacre.

Walk another block to King's Chapel (5) at the corner of Tremont and School Streets. The chapel was designed by Peter Harrison, who is known as America's First Architect. Never completed, the massive stone entrance tower was meant to rise to greater heights. Enter the church and view the well-preserved colonial interior. When founded in 1688 King's Chapel was the first Anglican church in New England. Later, its congregation separated from the Episcopal Church and became the first Unitarian Church in the United States. The churchyard, dating to 1630, is Boston's oldest: Governor Winthrop is buried here as is John Dawes, the man who accompanied Paul Revere on his midnight ride.

Walk down School Street. A statue of Benjamin

Franklin (6), by Richard Greenough, will be on your left. Franklin was born in Boston in 1706; his birthplace is farther along on the tour. In 1856, 150 years after Franklin's birth, this, the first portrait statue in Boston, was dedicated to his memory. The four panels at the statue's base depict chapters in Franklin's life: as a printer's apprentice, flying a kite as an electricity experiment, signing the Declaration of Independence, and preparing the Treaty of Paris, which ended the American Revolution. Nearby stands a statue of Josiah Quincy, Boston's mayor from 1823 to 1828. Quincy Market was the mayor's project and was later named in his memory. Both statues stand in front of Boston's old city hall. Built in 1862, the style is French Second Empire, a popular look for city halls at the time. Similar city halls stand in Philadelphia and in Providence, Rhode Island. When a newer city hall was built in Government Center in 1968, this building was converted for use as a restaurant.

School Street was the site of the first public school in America, a fact commemorated by a monument set in the pavement. The street ends at the Old Corner Bookstore (7). Built in 1712 as an apothecary, this is one of the oldest buildings in Boston. As a bookshop, it was frequented by such Boston literati as Oliver Wendell Holmes, Ralph Waldo Emerson, Nathaniel Hawthorne, and Henry Wadsworth Longfellow.

Make a right onto Washington Street. Your next stop is the Old South Meeting House (8). The first church to stand on this spot was a cedar structure (1670–1729). When the present building was completed in 1729 it was the largest indoor meeting place in the city and was used for assemblies prior to the American Rev-

Paul Revere and the Old North Church on the Freedom Trail

olution. The day after the Boston Massacre townspeople gathered here, as they did on December 13, 1773, the eve of the Boston Tea Party. This Congregational Church's worshipers moved to a newer church in Copley Square in the 1870s. The meeting house has since been preserved by the Old South Association.

From the meetinghouse walk just one block to 17 Milk Street and look at the bust of Benjamin Franklin that marks the place of his birth on January 17, 1706. He was baptized that same day in Old South Meeting House.

Retrace your steps down Washington Street, past the Old Corner Bookstore, and stop at the Old State House (9) at the end of Washington Street. Though the Old State House was built in 1713, this site was used as a public gathering place as far back as 1630. The town's first marketplace was here and later, in 1658, the town's first public building, the Town House, was erected in this vicinity. A fire destroyed much of Boston, including the Town House, in 1711. Construction of the present building began the following year. Note the balcony from which the Declaration of Independence was read on July 18, 1776. Above the balcony is a sundial flanked by the lion and the unicorn, symbols of British royalty. Step inside. Note the gallery, which provided a vantage point for the public to view and monitor proceedings on the floor. The Old State House is now a museum (617-720-1713, oldstatehouse@bostonhistory.org).

The Boston Massacre took place just outside the Old State House on March 5, 1770. The site is marked with a circular cobblestone memorial set in the pavement.

Walk down Congress Street to Faneuil Hall (10). En route to the hall you'll see the back of the new City Hall (1968) on your left. A massive block of concrete, the building faces a plaza that replaced the old Scully Square. A district of rundown theaters, bars, and tattoo parlors, Scully Square fell to the wrecking ball in the early 1960s and was replaced with today's Government Center.

Turn your attention to Dock Square and Faneuil Hall on your right. The site has been a marketplace since

1708. In 1749 a local Huguenot, Peter Faneuil, made a gift of the building to the city. It burned down and was replaced with an exact replica in 1762. Originally smaller, the hall was enlarged and transformed by Charles Bulfinch in 1805. He added a third story, widened the building from three to seven bays, and enclosed the previously open-air ground floor. Today Faneuil Hall remains, as it has always been, a multipurpose building. Shops occupy the ground floor; a meeting hall dubbed the Cradle of Liberty, because Samuel Adams and other patriots delivered inspiring speeches here, is on the second. A museum of the Ancient and Honorable Artillery Company occupies the uppermost level. Note the grasshopper weathervane atop the cupola—a symbol of Faneuil Hall and the adjacent marketplace.

The area now called Faneuil Hall Marketplace has long been known as Quincy Market. In 1824, Mayor Josiah Quincy proposed the buildings as an extension of Faneuil Hall. Alexander Parris designed the Greek Revival granite buildings. Renovated and updated in the 1970s, Faneuil Hall Marketplace has become a model for historic preservation projects and the adaptive reuse of older buildings. Where fishmongers, farmers, and merchants once peddled their goods more than a century ago, Bostonians and visitors alike now gather for eating, shopping, and entertainment.

The Freedom Trail's red line will next lead you down Union Street (11) and past the Blackstone Block, a remnant of the narrow, winding streets that were so typical in colonial Boston. Note the house at the corner of Union and Marshall Streets. It was built in about 1714. In 1798 the Duke of Chartres lodged here. He later became King Louis Phillippe of France. The Union

Oyster House has been here since 1826. It is said to be the oldest restaurant in continuous service in the nation. Daniel Webster was a frequent diner here, and a plaque upstairs marks John F. Kennedy's favorite booth.

Follow the red line to the North End and the Paul Revere House (12). One of Boston's oldest neighborhoods, the North End has been home to successive waves of immigrants: the Irish in the 1840s and '50s, and later Polish and Russian Jews. Today the North End is home to a large Italian community. Its restaurants, bakeries, pastry shops, butchers, and greengrocers line the streets in this, one of the city's most colorful and vibrant neighborhoods.

There are two reasons to visit the Paul Revere House. First, it is the oldest house standing in Boston (1680), and second, it was the home of one of the best-known patriots of the American Revolution. Revere was the descendant of Huguenots (French Protestants). He purchased this house in 1770 and lived here with his large family (he had 16 children). Other than the midnight ride immortalized in Longfellow's poem "Paul Revere's Ride" (1861), he is remembered for his bell foundry and as a silversmith. John Singleton Copley's portrait of Revere depicts him holding one of his silver teapots. Revere's cousin, Nathaniel Hichborn, lived in the brick house next door.

Follow the trail to Hanover Street—the North End's Main Street. St. Stephen's Church (13) will be on your right. Built in 1802–1804, this is Charles Bulfinch's only Boston church that still stands today. It was the New North Church (Unitarian), but was acquired by the Roman Catholic Archdiocese in 1862. On the

National Register of Historic Places, the church was restored in 1964.

Linking St. Stephen's with Old North Church is the Paul Revere Mall (14). The mall (*prado* to the locals) was created in 1933. Cyrus Dallin modeled the equestrian statue of Paul Revere in 1885, but it wasn't cast and mounted until 1940. At the far end of the mall, at 21 Unity Street, is the Clough House. Clough was the brick mason who built Old North Church. His house (1715) is one of the oldest in Boston and listed on the National Register of Historic Places.

Christ Church, popularly called the Old North Church (15), is historically significant for a number of reasons. It is best known for the two lanterns hung in its tower on April 18, 1775, to signal to Paul Revere that the British were coming. The episode was later immortalized in Longfellow's poem. This is the oldest church in Boston. Its peel's eight bells, cast in Gloucester, England, in 1744 are the oldest in the country. Designed by William Price in 1723, Christ Church was inspired by the earlier designs of London's Sir Christopher Wren. The elegant, three-tiered spire is the third to crown the tower. The first two were destroyed by hurricanes in 1804 and in 1954. The original weathervane, however, remains. Inside, note the high box pews, built to provide families with privacy and warmth on cold Sunday mornings. The brass candelabra have never been wired for electricity. In fact, Old North is lit solely by candlelight to this day (617-523-6676, church@oldnorth.com).

Walk to Copp's Hill Burying Ground (16), which dates to the 17th century. Across Boston's Inner Harbor is the Charlestown Navy Yard and the U.S.S. *Constitution*, which you will visit next.

Turn left onto Commercial Street and right onto North Washington Street. Cross the Charlestown Bridge. Charlestown, founded in 1628, was incorporated as a city in 1847 and annexed to the City of Boston in 1874. This makes Charlestown the oldest part of the City of Boston.

Once you're over the bridge and in Charlestown turn right onto Constitution Road to the Charlestown Navy Yard Visitor Center. The Navy Yard (17) was opened in 1800. Ships were built here and commissioned ships serviced and repaired. A part of Boston National Park, the Charlestown Navy Yard is administered by the National Park Service (617-242-5601, www.nps.gov/bost/bost).

Visit the U.S.S. *Constitution* (18). Commissioned in 1797, it is the world's oldest commissioned warship. Old Ironsides, as she is affectionately known, never lost a battle. The U.S.S. *Constitution* Museum documents the ship's history through art, artifacts, and interactive exhibits.

For the final leg of the Freedom Trail leave the Navy Yard through Gate Four and follow the red line, which will lead you up Tremont Street to the Bunker Hill Monument (19). This is not Bunker, but Breed's Hill, on June 16, 1775, the site of the first major battle of the American Revolution. The cornerstone for the Quincy granite obelisk was laid by the Marquis de Lafayette in 1825. Completed in 1843, the monument stands 220 feet tall. Visitors may climb to the top and enjoy a panoramic view of Boston Harbor, the Mystic River, the Charles River, and the cities and towns beyond. A multimedia presentation, *The Whites of Their Eyes,* is offered at the base of the monument, as is a small museum.

Note, also, the statue of Colonel William Prescott, who commanded the American troops at the battle.

Option A: You may continue on the Freedom Trail down Monument and Winthrop Streets. This will take you by Town Hill (site of the original settlement in 1629) and John Harvard Mall. The mall is named for an English minister who died in 1638, leaving his library and half his fortune to the newly founded school that was later named for him: Harvard College. The trail then retraces its route across the Charlestown Bridge and back to Boston.

Option B: Return to the Charlestown Navy Yard. Harbor Cruises operates the Inner Harbor ferry between Pier #4 and Boston's Long Wharf, which is close to Faneuil Hall Marketplace. For ferry information contact 617-227-4321, www.mbta.com.

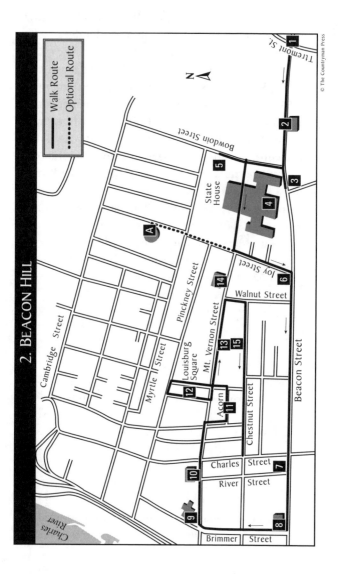

2 · Beacon Hill

Directions: *By car:* Park at or near the Boston Common Garage. Call 617-954-2096 for directions to the garage from all points. *By public transportation:* Take the T Green or Red Line to Park Street, or take the Blue or Green Line to Government Center (1-800-392-6100, www.mbta.com).

Begin your tour at the foot of Beacon Hill, at the corner (1) of Beacon and Tremont Streets. Tremont was named for the three hills on which much of Boston was built: Mount Vernon, Pemberton Hill, and Beacon Hill. Two of the hills were leveled in the 19th century; only Beacon Hill remains.

Start your ascent up the hill on Beacon Street. Your first stop is the Boston Athenaeum (2) which will be on your left at #10½. The Athenaeum was founded in 1807 as a library and art museum. In 1870 the art collection formed the nucleus of the Boston Museum of Fine Arts. Today the athenaeum remains a private, or proprietary, library. The building was completed in 1849. Its architect, Edward Clark Cabot, was heavily influenced by the work of the Italian Renaissance architect Andrea Palladio. The large, vaulted reading room was added in the following century by architect Henry Forbes Bigelow. For information about touring the athenaeum call 617-227-0270 (www.bostonatheneum.org).

Continue your climb up Beacon Hill. Number 16 will be on the left. A Federal House built in 1808 by Thomas Fletcher, it is a national historic landmark.

Stop at the corner of Beacon and Park Streets. The red brick building on the corner is the Amory Ticknor House (3). Note the elegant, curved stairway and columned portico facing Park Street. Designed by Charles Bulfinch in 1803, this was the largest, finest Federal mansion in Boston when it was built for merchant Thomas Amory. Altered and divided later in the 19th century, the mansion is today a shadow of its former self and houses shops and offices.

Turn and face the State House (1795). The starting point of the Freedom Trail, the House (4) is described elsewhere in this guide (see page 18). Walk down Bowdoin Street to the right of the State House. You'll walk past the building's granite wings, added in 1914. The yellow brick annex in the rear was added in 1889–1895. As you walk down Bowdoin Street the Beacon Hill Memorial (5) will be on your left. A 60-foot high Doric column with an eagle perched on top, the present memorial (1898) replicates an earlier (1790) monument designed by Charles Bulfinch. The column marks the spot where a wooden pole stood from 1634 until 1789, which carried a beacon to warn townsfolk of emergencies, hence the name of the hill.

Backtrack just a few steps to Mount Vernon Street and walk through the arch and under the State House annex to Joy Street.

Option A: To visit the Museum of Afro-American History turn right onto Joy Street. The museum will be on your left at 8 Smith Court. It includes the African

American Meeting House (the oldest in the nation) and the Abiel Smith School (the first publicly funded grammar school for black children in America). Maps are available for a self-guided Black Heritage Trail walking tour (617-725-0022).

Walk down Joy Street (named for Benjamin Joy, an early 19th-century developer) and return to Beacon Street. The house (6) at the intersection with Walnut Street (#1 Walnut Street) is an 1804 Bulfinch design and the birthplace of the abolitionist Wendell Phillips.

Continue your walk down Beacon Street as far as Brimmer Street. En route you'll pass many notable early 19th-century homes.

The Greek Revival houses at 39 and 40 Beacon were designed by Alexander Parris in 1818. Henry Wadsworth Longfellow married resident Fanny Appleton here. Later these served as the clubhouses for the Women's City Club.

The granite structure at 42 Beacon has twin bow fronts facing the street. The bow front on the right is the older of the two. It was built by Alexander Parris in 1819 for Col. David Sears. The second bow was added in 1832. Since 1872 this has been the Somerset Club. An interesting aside: The home of colonial American artist John Singleton Copley once stood on this site.

The third Harrison Gray Otis House, at 45 Beacon Street, was built in 1805. Charles Bulfinch had also designed the first Harrison Gray Otis House (at 141 Cambridge Street, see page 55) and the second (at 85 Mount Vernon Street, which appears later on this tour). Note the cobblestone courtyard and the carriage house. The house is now headquarters for the American Meteorological Society.

The two Asher Benjamin houses at 54 and 55 Beacon display many Greek Revival details. Number 55 is the Prescott House. It is open to the public and maintained by the National Society of the Colonial Dames of America in the Commonwealth of Massachusetts (617-742-3190).

Four Ephraim Marsh houses are next. Numbers 56 and 57 are Federal style, built in 1819; the other two (numbers 63 and 64) are Greek Revival, built in the 1820s. The latter are the King's Chapel parish house. Note the purple windowpanes imported from England and glazed into place around 1824.

Continue down Beacon Street, crossing Charles Street. The banks of the Charles River originally ran along what is now Charles Street. The Public Garden on the left is included in the Back Bay walking tour (see page 37). On the right is a row of granite houses (numbers 70–75) designed by Benjamin Asher in 1828. A few doors farther on is Hampshire House Restaurant (8). Peek through the wrought iron fence to the Bull and Finch Pub downstairs. This pub was the inspiration for the TV comedy series *Cheers*.

Leave Beacon Street, turning right onto Brimmer. Stop at the corner of Mount Vernon Street. The Church of the Advent (9) is across the way. An Episcopal parish founded in 1844, The Advent brought the Oxford Movement from the Church of England to this side of the Atlantic. The church was designed and built for Anglo-Catholic worship, featuring an ample apse with a high altar and reredos for solemn high mass on Sunday and greater feast days, and a series of smaller chapels and shrines for weekday low masses and devotions. The style is Victorian High Gothic, the architects

The Public Garden

Sturgis and Brigham (1875). The Lady Chapel interior (1894) was designed by American medievalist Ralph Adams Cram. The bell tower houses exceptionally fine English bells. Visitors may ascend the steps of the tower to watch a team of volunteers during "change ringing," done before Sunday high mass. A July Fourth tradition: The Advent's bells are rung as part of the Boston Pops' performance of Tchaikovsky's *1812 Overture* (617-523-2377, www.theadvent.org).

Turn right onto Mount Vernon Street. Note the yellow cottage on the right at number 130. This enchanting little house was built in 1840 and is known as the Sunflower Cottage because of the decorative motif under the gable.

The little firehouse across Mt. Vernon Street was used in the 1980s TV series *Spenser for Hire.* Robert Urich played the title role—a detective whose apartment was in this firehouse.

Next is the Charles Street Meeting House (10). Built in 1804 by Asher Benjamin for the Third Baptist Church, this later became the African Methodist Episcopal Church and was later used by Unitarian Universalists. While the exterior has retained its original character, the interior was renovated in 1982 to house shops and offices. Another, similar Benjamin church, the Old West Church, survives on the other side of Beacon Hill (see page 56).

Cross Charles Street and begin your ascent back up Beacon Hill along Mount Vernon Street. The diminutive Cedar Lane Way will be on the left. Continue to walk up Mount Vernon Street, turn right onto West Cedar Street, and then left onto Acorn (11). Walk the length of Acorn Street, said to be the most photographed in America. The little houses along the way were once homes to coachmen who worked for wealthier folks living on Beacon Street and Louisburg Square.

At the end of Acorn turn left onto Willow Street and then explore Louisburg Square (12). Developed in 1826 on the site of the leveled Mount Vernon, the houses were built in the 1830s and '40s. Louisa May Alcott lived at number 10. The park has statues of Christopher Columbus and Aristides. Both were placed here in 1850 by a Greek merchant who lived on the square.

Return to Mount Vernon Street and resume your walk up the hill. The houses at numbers 70 and 72 were designed by Richard Upjohn in 1847. These later housed Boston University's School of Theology, then apartments, and now condominiums.

Both numbers 85 and 87 are Bulfinch Houses. Eighty-five is the second Harrison Gray Otis House (1800).

Next cross the street to a row of humbler dwellings, numbers 50 through 60 (13). These were built to serve as stables for the Swan Houses on Chestnut Street by Bulfinch in 1804. You will see the Swan Houses later on this tour.

The Nichols House Museum (14) is at 55 Mount Vernon Street. Another Charles Bulfinch design, it was built in 1804. In 1885 the house was acquired by the family of Rose Standish Nichols, who lived here for the next 75 years. When she died in 1960 at the age of 88 she willed that her house be opened to the public as a museum. Offering an unusual and wonderful glimpse of life on Beacon Hill, the house is filled with Nichols family furniture, decorative arts, and memorabilia, some of which dates to the 16th century (617-227-6993, www.nichols-housemuseum.org).

From Mount Vernon Street walk down Walnut Street and then turn right onto Chestnut Street. On the right (numbers 13, 15, 17) are the Swan Houses (15). Built as wedding gifts for three daughters of Mrs. Hepzibah Swan, the row was designed by Bulfinch in 1804. The Bulfinch houses opposite (numbers 6 and 8) are contemporary with the Swan Houses and are now occupied by the Society of Friends (Quakers). Note the curved stairway, similar to Bulfinch's stairway at the Amory Ticknor House earlier in this tour. The Gothic Revival building at 27 Chestnut Street, designed by the firm-Bellows, Aldrich & Holt in 1917, was contiguous with Boston University's School of Theology, seen earlier on Mount Vernon Street. It now houses condominiums.

Continue down Chestnut street. A plaque on the facade of number 50 identifies this as the home of historian and author Francis Parkman. Next door, number 52, was the home or Ralph Adams Cram, architect, prolific writer, and medievalist. Across the street the Harvard Musical Association's clubhouse and concert hall occupies the 1827 building at 57A. The walking tour of Beacon Hill ends just a few steps away on Charles Street.

3 · Back Bay

Directions: *By car:* Park at or near the Boston Common Garage. Call 617-954-2096 for directions to the garage from all points.
By public transportation: Take the T Green Line to Arlington Street (1-800-392-6100, www.mbta.com).

This tour begins, appropriately, at the first building erected in the Back Bay: the Arlington Street Church (1). Facing the front door of the church is a statue of William Ellery Channing: abolitionist, founder of the Unitarian movement in the United States, and a minister at this church. The church was built between 1859 and 1861 according to designs by Arthur Gilman who based this work on an English prototype: St. Martin-in-the-Fields, London. (617-536-7050, http://world.std.com/~ascuua/).

Walk down Arlington Street. The Ritz Carlton Hotel (2) will be on your left. It was built in 1931; a second building mirroring the first was added a half-century later. Commonwealth Avenue begins at the next corner, its earliest houses dating to 1861. Cross Arlington Street and enter the Boston Public Garden (3). There has been a garden on this site since 1839. The paths were laid out in 1859, and the small suspension footbridge and the fence enclosing the garden were added

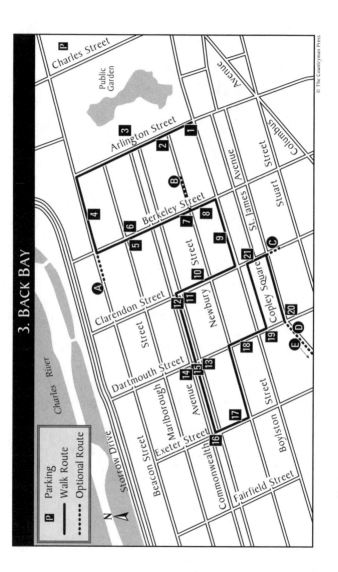

3. BACK BAY

Legend:
- P — Parking
- —— Walk Route
- ••••• Optional Route

N

Charles River

Storrow Drive

Beacon Street

Marlborough Street

Commonwealth Avenue

Newbury Street

Boylston Street

Public Garden

Charles Street

Arlington Street

Berkeley Street

Clarendon Street

Dartmouth Street

Exeter Street

Fairfield Street

St. James Avenue

Stuart Street

Columbus Avenue

Copley Square

© The Countryman Press

in 1861. The equestrian statue of George Washington was modeled by Thomas Ball and dedicated in 1869. Cross the footbridge to the dock where the swan boats embark. The Paget family has owned and paddled the swan boats since 1877.

Return to Arlington Street and continue toward Beacon Street. Note the rows of brownstone houses with mansard roofs. Built starting in the 1860s, these French Second Empire–style homes fill much of the Back Bay. Make a left on Beacon Street, which runs on the site of the old Mill Dam, placed here in the 1850s, that effectively enclosed the Back Bay. The bay was later filled with tons of gravel brought by rail from Needham, Massachusetts. Boston's newest and most fashionable 19th-century neighborhood was thus created.

The Gibson House Museum, at 137 Beacon Street (4), was built in 1860 and is a well-preserved Back Bay Victorian house today. Tours of the museum allow today's visitors a glimpse at a typical 19th-century Back Bay house. The museum is also the headquarters for the New England chapter of the Victorian Society (617-267-6338, www.thegibsonhouse.org).

On leaving the Gibson House make a left and walk to Berkeley Street.

Option A: Another Back Bay townhouse open to the public is just a few doors away at number 170, an Ogden Codman design. Codman was an architect and interior designer who preferred 18th-century decor over dark, cluttered Victorian interiors. Noted author Edith Wharton collaborated with Codman on a book entitled *The Decoration of Houses.* Published in 1897, it is still in print today (W. W. Norton). The house's sandstone exterior is Renaissance Revival, while its interior is 18th-century

English. The house is now the headquarters for the Goethe Institute and the German Cultural Center (617-262-6050, www.goethe.de/uk/bos/englisch/enallg.htm).

Walk down Berkeley and stop at Marlborough Street. The First and Second Church (5) will be across Marlborough Street on the right. The congregation, one of the oldest in the country, became Unitarian in the 19th century. An English Gothic Revival church was built here in 1867. After most of it burned in 1968 the gutted interior was replaced with a more modern structure, designed by Paul Rudolph. The statue of Governor John Winthrop, modeled by Richard Greenough in 1880, stood in the old Scully Square until 1903 when it was moved to this, a more dignified setting.

The First Lutheran Church (6), designed by Pietro Belluschi, is on your left. On approaching the church you are greeted by a quiet, enclosed garden—a refuge in the city. While the church design is innovative, it is widely thought to be out of place among its Victorian neighbors.

Continue down Berkeley Street, cross Commonwealth Avenue again, and stop at the corner of Newbury Street in front of the Church of the Covenant (7). Founded in 1835 as Central Congregational Church, the congregation moved from its South End church in 1865. Richard M. Upjohn, whose father designed Trinity Church on Wall Street in New York City, followed in his father's footsteps by designing this, a Gothic Revival church. The building material is Roxbury puddingstone. Note the majestic, lofty spire that rises over 235 feet. The interior is lit by a series of Tiffany windows. The focus of the sanctuary is a large hanging Tiffany lamp that is surrounded by winged angels.

Made in 1893, the lamp was unveiled at the Colombian Exposition in Chicago.

On the right, across Newbury Street, is a French Academic red brick building (8) set back from the streets on all sides. This housed the New England Museum of Natural History from 1864 until the Boston Museum of Science replaced it in the early 1950s. Both museums had their roots in the Boston Society of Natural History, which was founded in 1830. Today the former museum building is a clothing store.

Option B: The Leslie Lindsey Memorial Chapel is on Newbury Street midway between Arlington and Berkeley Streets. An adjunct to Emmanuel Episcopal Church (built in 1862 and expanded in 1899), the chapel was dedicated in 1924 by the parents of Leslie Lindsey, who perished on the *Lusitania* in World War I. The architects were Allen and Collins, whose most famous work is Riverside Church in New York City. The chapel occupies a long, narrow space. Its Gothic vaulting, however, soars. The high altar and stained-glass windows were designed by Englishman Sir Ninian Comper. Note the outstanding ornamental ironwork. Though small, all the details combine to make this a remarkably beautiful chapel.

Continue on Berkeley Street and turn right onto Boylston Street, which was named for Boston physician Dr. Zabdiel Boylston, the first in America to vaccinate against smallpox (1720). The massive granite office building on your right, completed in 1942 as the New England Mutual Life Insurance Company Building (9), is now New England Financial's headquarters (617-578-2000). Surprisingly, this was designed by the firm of Cram and Ferguson, better known for their Gothic

Revival churches and collegiate buildings. It stands on the first site of the Massachusetts Institute of Technology (1866), which moved across the Charles River to Cambridge in 1916. Inside the lobby at 501 Boylston Street is a series of eight murals depicting scenes from Massachusetts colonial history and four delightful dioramas illustrating this very site at various points in history: 2,500 B.C. (an Indian fishweir), 1625 (within sight of the William Blaxton house), 1858 (the filling of the Back Bay), and 1863 (construction of the Boston Society of Natural History building).

When you leave the New England Financial building turn right onto Boylston Street and at the next corner right again onto Clarendon Street. At the corner of Clarendon and Newbury Streets is Trinity Church's rectory (10). Built by Henry Hobson Richardson in 1879, this is an excellent example of "Richardsonian Romanesque." Note Richardson's signature arch at the entryway, not unlike those at Sever Hall at Harvard University and Crane Memorial Library in Quincy.

Walk along Clarendon Street one block to Commonwealth Avenue. The First Baptist Church (11) will be on the left. Another H. H. Richardson work, this was his first Romanesque Revival church, built for the Brattle Square Unitarian congregation in 1870. It was later acquired by the First Baptist Church. Certainly the church's most outstanding feature is its freestanding bell tower, which emulates an Italian campanile. Note the angels blowing their horns from each corner of the tower. Boston is "Beantown" and the church is known as the Church of the Holy Bean Blowers. The angels form a part of a frieze surrounding the tower. The frieze was modeled by Frédéric-Auguste Bartholdi, whose

GREATER BOSTON CONVENTION & VISITORS' BUREAU

Trinity Church and the John Hancock Tower, Copley Square

most famous work is the Statue of Liberty. Like the Church of the Covenant, this is built of Roxbury puddingstone.

Turn left onto Commonwealth Avenue and walk

down the center of the mall past the monument to Patrick Andrew Collins (12), who was Boston's mayor from 1902 through 1905. Next you'll see the monument dedicated to the nine firefighters who lost their lives in the Hotel Vendome fire on June 17, 1972. The Hotel Vendome (13) is just ahead on the left. Built in the French Second Empire style in the 1870s and 1880s, this was Boston's most fashionable hotel and hosted many notables, including four presidents. Following the devastating fire the Vendome was converted to condominiums.

Opposite the Vendome, to the right, is the Ames-Webster Mansion (14), arguably Back Bay's most opulent house. The 1872 Peabody and Stearns mansion was enlarged by John Sturgis ten years later. It houses offices today.

Continue down Commonwealth Avenue Mall. Stop at the statue of the seated William Lloyd Garrison (15). A Bostonian and a leading abolitionist who lived from 1805 to 1879, his monument bears one of his strongest statements: "I am in earnest. I will not equivocate. I will not excuse. I will not retreat a single inch, and I will be heard."

Walk one more block to Exeter Street and a monument depicting a relaxed Samuel Eliot Morison (16) perched on a rock. Morison, who lived from 1887 to 1976, was a life-long Bostonian, an admiral, and an historian. Turn left onto Exeter Street. The Exeter Theatre (17) will be on the left. Another Richardsonian Romanesque building, this was erected in 1884 as the First Spiritualist Temple. In 1913 it was converted for use as a movie theater and, in 1985, became a retail store.

Turn left onto Newbury Street and then right onto Dartmouth Street. Copley Square High School will be on the right. Built as the Boston Art Club in 1881, it was designed by William Ralph Emerson (nephew of the poet) in the Queen Anne Revival style in 1881.

Next door, at the corner of Dartmouth and Boylston Streets, is the New Old South Church (18). The successor to the Old South Meeting House on the Freedom Trail (see page 20), it was built in 1874 according to plans by Cummings and Sears in the Northern Italian Gothic Revival style. Note the central lantern over the nave and the campanile, which towers nearly 250 feet. This became Boston's "leaning tower" early in the last century and was dismantled and then rebuilt in 1940. The stunning interior was restored in 1985.

You have reached Copley Square, named in honor of Boston native and artist John Singleton Copley (1737–1815). For many years Copley Square was divided by intersecting Huntington Avenue into two pie wedges. The flowerbeds of the old Copley Square were replaced by a rectangular concrete plaza in 1969. The present park setting was adopted in the early 1980s. The Boston Public Library (19) is ahead on the right. Founded in 1848, it was the first public library in a major American city. The library building facing Copley Square was designed by Charles F. McKim, of McKim, Mead, and White, in 1887 and is based on Italian Renaissance palazzi. Before entering, note the huge wrought-iron lanterns flanking the entrance doors. Then turn around and see how these frame the view of Copley Square and Trinity Church. Walk past the wrought-iron gates and the bronze doors modeled by Daniel Chester French. They represent truth and romance, knowledge and wisdom, and music and poetry. Once inside, ascend the grand staircase and enter the main reading room, called Bates Hall—named for the library's first benefactor. The massive, vaulted room runs the width of the building—over 200 feet. The adjacent room is embellished with a pre-Raphaelite-style mural, *The Quest for the Holy Grail.* Ascend the stair one more flight and view a remarkable series of murals by John Singer Sargent titled *Judaism and Christianity.* A wing was added to the library in 1971 (Philip Johnson, architect). Between the wings is a peaceful garden and courtyard surrounded by cloister walks, where chairs have been placed. Inspired by a Roman palace's courtyard, this is a true refuge from the noise and hurried pace of the city (617-536-5400, www.bpl.org).

Leave the library through the Copley Square doors. The Fairmont Copley Plaza Hotel (20) is on the right. Designed in 1910, the hotel stands on the former site of the Boston Museum of Fine Arts (from 1876 to 1909).

Walk across Copley Square to Trinity Church (21). This Episcopal parish was founded in 1734 and for many years worshiped in its Summer Street church in downtown Boston. Like so many downtown churches, Trinity followed its parishioners to the newly filled and fashionable Back Bay in the 1870s. Impressed by his design for the First Baptist (Brattle) Church seen earlier on this tour, the Trinity congregation invited Henry Hobson Richardson to design their new church. This is considered Richardson's greatest work. The Richardsonian Romanesque church was complete in 1877; the portico and front towers were added in 1890. Visit the interior, which is lit by Tiffany windows. The interior of the expansive central tower is embellished with frescoes by

John LaFarge. A cloister walk containing a Gothic window tracery from St. Botolph's church in Boston, England, connects the church and its parish house. Trinity's best-known rector was Phillips Brooks, the author of the Christmas carol "O Little Town of Bethlehem." A monument to Brooks stands outside the church, facing Boylston Street. The statue was modeled by Augustus Saint-Gaudens, and the niche behind it was designed by McKim, Mead, and White (617-536-0944, www.trinitychurchboston.org).

Option C: To see a bird's eye view of Back Bay take the elevator to the observation room on top of the John Hancock Tower next to Trinity Church. Designed by I. M. Pei, the tower was completed in 1975. It overshadows the John Hancock Building (1947, Cram and Ferguson, architects). An interesting aside: The lights on the older building's cupola have been forecasting the weather for generations of Bostonians who are familiar with the rhyme:

> *Clear blue, clear view;*
> *Flashing blue, clouds are due;*
> *Steady red, rain ahead;*
> *Flashing red, snow instead.*

Option D: Wedged between the Copley Plaza Hotel and the Boston Public Library is the Westin Hotel. A skybridge connects the Westin to Copley Place, a vast indoor mall (1980, the Architects Collaborative). Another skybridge connects Copley Place with the Prudential Center. When built in 1959, The Pru was a symbol of "the new Boston." Not to be outdone by Copley Place, the Prudential Center has been expanded and updated.

Option E: Huntington Avenue starts between the Boston Public Library and the Westin Hotel. A walk down Huntington will take you by the Prudential Center and then to the Christian Science Church Center. Walk the length of the reflecting pool at the Church Center. The present Center, designed by architects I. M. Pei along with Cossuta and Ponte in the early 1970s, incorporates older buildings such as the Mother Church Extension, which resembles a large Italian Renaissance basilica, and the Mapparium. Located in the Publishing Society Building, the Mapparium is an enormous multicolored glass globe, complete with oceans, countries, and other geographic details. Visitors walk through the center of the Mapparium on a footbridge.

Neighboring the Church Center, at the intersections of Massachusetts and Huntington Avenues, are two buildings worth noting. Symphony Hall, a McKim, Mead, and White design, is a Renaissance Revival work completed in 1900. Its acoustics are impeccable. Home to the Boston Symphony and Boston Pops Orchestras, Symphony Hall also hosts visiting world-class performing artists (617-266-1492). Horticultural Hall (1901, Wheelright and Haven, architects) stands on Massachusetts Avenue opposite Symphony Hall.

4 · The Charles River and MIT

Directions: *By car:* Park at or near the Boston Common Garage. Call 617-954-2096 for directions to the garage from all points. *By public transportation:* Take the T Green Line to Arlington Street or the Red Line to Charles Street (1-800-392-6100, www.mbta.com).

This walk begins at the corner of Beacon and Arlington Streets (1). Take the Arthur Fiedler Footbridge over Storrow Drive to the banks of the Charles River. When you arrive at the river look to your right to the Hatch Shell (2). The shell was built in 1940 as a memorial to Edward Hatch and was renovated and updated fifty years later. Arthur Fiedler conducted the first July Fourth Boston Pops concert in 1929 and continued the tradition until his death fifty years later. The footbridge named for him was built in 1954. There is a larger-than-life bust of the legendary conductor on this walk. The highlight of every summer season at the Hatch Shell remains the July Fourth concert, which always culminates with Tchaikovsky's *1812 Overture* and the sound of howitzers, the peal of The Advent's church bells, and the sight of fireworks overhead.

As you face the river a small footbridge crossing a lagoon to an island is on the left. Cross the bridge and turn left, walking parallel to the river. The landscaping,

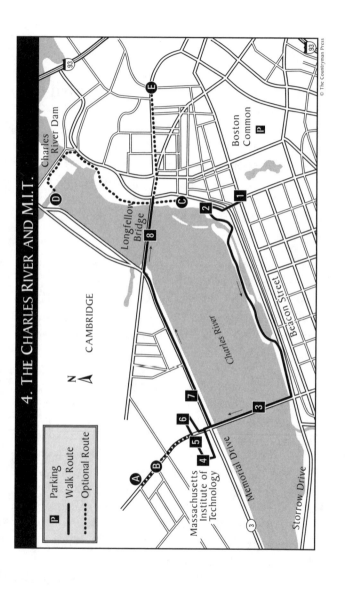

4. THE CHARLES RIVER AND M.I.T.

P Parking
⎯⎯ Walk Route
······ Optional Route

N

CAMBRIDGE

Massachusetts
Institute of
Technology

Memorial Drive

Storrow Drive

Charles River

Charles
River Dam

Longfellow Bridge

Boston
Common

Beacon Street

93

93

3

© The Countryman Press

footbridges, and lagoons so many enjoy today were added in 1931 as the Storrow Memorial Embankment, given in memory of banker James J. Storrow by his wife. The Storrow Memorial Drive was completed in 1951, effectively separating the park and river from Back Bay. Continue walking along the Charles River. En route are sweeping views of the Massachusetts Institute of Technology (MIT) campus across the river in Cambridge. MIT was founded in 1861 by William Barton Rogers. At first the school was located in Boston's Copley Square. In 1916 it moved to its 135-acre site in Cambridge, where much of its campus stretches along the river's edge.

As you look toward MIT you'll see the dome which sits atop the Baker Engineering Library. Modeled after the Pantheon in Rome, it was designed by William Welles Bosworth in 1913. The architectural style of the library and the adjacent buildings can best be described "restrained beaux-arts."

At Massachusetts Avenue walk up the ramp to Harvard Bridge (3) and cross the bridge to Cambridge. First built in 1887, the bridge was reconstructed a century later. A plaque on the right side of the bridge marks the spot where Harry Houdini performed a daring escape in the waters below in 1908. The curious markers at intervals on the bridge are "smoots" painted by MIT fraternity pledges. As you approach MIT you'll see that its campus is on both sides of Massachusetts Avenue. Once in Cambridge turn left and walk to the large, triangular Kresge Auditorium (4). Interestingly, its outer shell, one-eighth of a sphere, is free-floating and touches the ground in only three corners. The auditorium and theater within do not touch the outer shell. Next visit the

Kresge Chapel (5). Both the chapel and the auditorium were designed by Eero Saarinen in 1955. A brick cylinder, the chapel's interior is beautiful in its utter simplicity. Harry Bertoia's braised steel reredos behind the altar is lit by a skylight. On the exterior, the chapel's 45-foot high bell tower was designed by Theodore Roszak. Facing both auditorium and chapel is the Julius Adams Stratton Building, designed by Eduardo Catalano in 1965. It serves as MIT's student center.

Cross the street to 77 Massachusetts Avenue, known as the Rogers Building or Building 7. At the Information Center (6) a map is available that indicates the location of artwork on campus. MIT is dotted with sculptures by Alexander Calder, Henry Moore, Louise Nevelson, and others.

Option A: The MIT Museum is at 265 Massachusetts Avenue and permanently displays MIT memorabilia and exhibits on science and technology (617-253-4444, http://web.mit.edu/museum/).

Option B: The Hart Nautical Gallery, at 33 Massachusetts Avenue, has one of the most significant collections of nautical materials in America (617-253-5942, http://web.mit/edu/).

From the Information Center walk down the corridor to Building 7's lobby (the A Lobby), turn right, and enter the Infinite Corridor. While not infinite, the corridor is certainly long—one-sixth of a mile to be exact—just one link in the seven miles of halls that connect MIT's buildings. Retrace your steps and walk through Building 3 to Building 10 and take the elevator to the fifth floor, where you will be under the dome of the Baker Engineering Library. This is the dome viewed earlier on the tour from across the river. Descend to the first floor and visit the Compton Gallery. Karl Taylor Compton was MIT's president from 1930 to 1949; this gallery is dedicated to his wife and features changing exhibits of interest to MIT and the wider community. Be sure to visit the MIT timeline exhibit, which documents the period from 1845 to the near-present. The 30-foot-long, permanent exhibit runs between the Compton Gallery and the Building 10 lobby.

Exit at Massachusetts Avenue, turn left, and make another left onto Memorial Drive along the river. Take another look at the Baker Library. The vast lawn in front is known as Killian Court. On the left is Henry Moore's bronze *Three Piece Reclining Figure, Draped* (1976). On the right is a work on loan from New York's Metropolitan Museum of Art. The eleven-piece granite sculpture *Guennette* was created by Michael Heizer in 1977.

Sit on one of the benches (7) facing the Charles and enjoy the unrivaled, sweeping view of Boston's skyline. Try to identify some of Boston's outstanding landmarks. From right to left: the Citgo sign in Kenmore Square near Fenway Park, the Prudential Center, the John Hancock Building and Tower, and Beacon Hill (note the gilded dome atop Bulfinch's 1795 State House and the cluster of skyscrapers in the financial district).

Resume your walk. The stone bridge ahead is the Longfellow Bridge (8), known to Bostonians as the "salt- and pepper-shaker bridge" because of its towers. The first bridge to span the Charles at this spot was built in 1793. The present bridge was completed in 1907, according to plans by Edmund March Wheelwright. Interestingly, Wheelwright's design was inspired by a bridge he had seen in St. Petersburg, Russia. Why the name Longfellow? The poet frequently traveled across the original bridge to and from his Cambridge home.

Walk across the bridge and return to Boston. Stop along the way to enjoy a closer look at Beacon Hill. On the right note the spire of the Church of the Advent (1875). To the left is the Museum of Science. The museum appears to be sitting in the middle of the river. In fact, it sits at a dam, completed in 1910, that replaced an earlier bridge (1809). The dam's gates are opened periodically, and so on one day the Charles River basin may appear to be calm and lakelike, and the next day it will flow as a river should. Science Park runs parallel to the dam. Today's Museum of Science is the successor to the Boston Society of Natural History (1830). The Society's museum was in Back Bay on Berkeley Street between Boylston and Newbury Streets. The old museum building still stands and has been converted to a clothing store. The present Museum of Science was built in 1951 and has grown over the years with addition of new galleries, the Charles Hayden Planetarium, and the Mugar Omnimax Theater. In the distance to the left you'll see the Leonard P. Zakim Bunker Hill Bridge. Completed in 2002, the bridge is part of the Big Dig and links Boston with Charlestown. Its twin 270-foot-high towers echo the design of Charlestown's Bunker Hill Monument. When you arrive in Boston you have several choices.

Option C: Return to the Esplanade along the river and complete a full circle, returning to the Arthur Fiedler footbridge.

Option D: Walk along the river in the opposite direction and visit Science Park and its attractions (617-723-2500, www.mos.org).

Option E: A walk down Cambridge Street will lead

The Charles River from MIT

you to four significant sites. The Charles Street Jail was built in 1850 of Quincy granite and utilized as a prison until 1991. It was renovated for use by Massachusetts General Hospital as a clinic and into retail and hotel space. Massachusetts General Hospital was founded in 1811; its oldest and most historic building is Bullfinch's Pavilion. The granite Federal-style pavilion was completed in 1821. At its center is the Ether Dome. Here on October 16, 1846, ether was used as an anesthetic in surgery for the first time. The dome is open to visitors and has a mummy, a skeleton, and 19th-century surgical instruments on display. The red brick house at the corner of Cambridge and North Grove Streets was the Resident Physician's House, built in 1891 and moved to this site in 1981 (617-726-2206).

The Harrison Gray Otis House is a little farther down Cambridge Street at the corner of Lynde Street. Otis, at one time mayor of Boston, commissioned Charles Bulfinch to design this spacious, elegant house. The plain brick exterior belies the sumptuous interior, decorated with the finest furnishings of the period and imported carpets and wallpapers. Opened to visitors by the Society for the Preservation of New England Antiquities, the building also contains the society's library and archives (over a million photos, drawings, and other documents) (617-227-3956, www.spnea.org).

Old West Church is next door to the Otis House. There has been a church on this site since 1737. The first church (used as barracks by the British during the Revolution) was replaced by the present church, Federal in style, in 1806. The architect was Asher Benjamin. When many church members moved elsewhere in the late 19th century the church closed. Old West was used as a branch of the Boston Public Library from 1896 to 1960. In 1964 it was restored and reopened as a church. In 1971 a new Fisk organ was installed and dedicated; it is considered the finest instrument of its genre in the nation. Originally Congregational, Old West is now a member of the United Methodist Church (617-227-5088, www.oldwestchurch.org).

As you walk down Cambridge Street you're passing the old West End (from Cambridge Street to the river). Once a vibrant neighborhood and home to many immigrants, including the Irish, Italians, Jews, Poles, and Russians, the entire West End fell to the wrecking ball in 1958 by orders of the Boston Redevelopment Authority. The project has been universally acknowledged as a disaster performed under the guise of "urban renewal," and the loss of the old West End is widely lamented.

5 · Harvard and Old Cambridge

Directions: *By car:* From Boston, cross the Charles River to Cambridge on the Charles River Dam, Longfellow Bridge, or Harvard Bridge. Drive west on US 3. At Harvard University turn right onto John. F. Kennedy Street to Harvard Square. *By public transportation:* Take the T Red Line to Harvard (1-800-392-6100, www.mbta.com).

Newtowne (as the city was first named) was settled in 1630 by members of the Massachusetts Bay Company. Six years later a college opened which we now know as Harvard—named for John Harvard, who bequeathed his library and half his fortune to the budding school. Newtowne became Cambridge, in emulation of the English university town. The city has grown to a population hovering near 100,000, but this walk will concentrate on the colonial town and the university.

Begin the tour in Harvard Square (1). With your back to the newspaper kiosk face Harvard Yard. Note Wadsworth House (2), the yellow clapboard house on the right. Enter the Yard through the gate to the left of Wadworth House (617-495-1000, www.harvard.edu).

Wadsworth House was built in 1727 for Harvard's eighth president, Benjamin Wadsworth. George Washington used the house as his headquarters for a time in

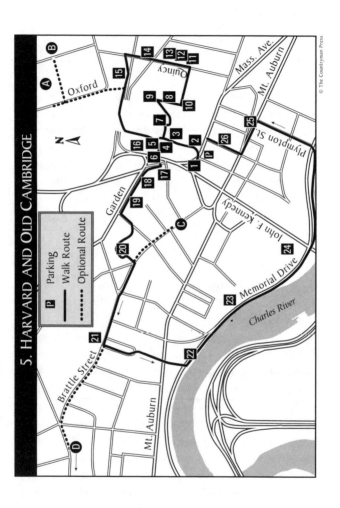

5. HARVARD AND OLD CAMBRIDGE

P Parking
—— Walk Route
······· Optional Route

© The Countryman Press

1775. The building now houses university offices.

Continue straight ahead into the Old Yard (3). The dormitories surrounding it are used for freshman housing. After their first year Harvard undergraduates join one of the houses on campus and live in that house until graduation. There are several undergraduate houses along the route of this tour.

The red brick Massachusetts Hall (4) will be on the left. Built in 1720, it is the oldest Harvard building standing today. Constructed for use as a dormitory and used as a barracks for the Continental Army during the American Revolution, it is now used as office space for the university's chief officers.

Harvard Hall (5) faces Massachusetts Hall. Built in 1766, it replaced the first hall which stood on the site (1677). That building, along with John Harvard's library, burned in 1764.

Both Massachusetts and Harvard Hall flank the Johnston Gate (6). Though the gate dates to 1890, it stands on the spot that has been the main entrance to the yard since the 17th century.

With your back to Johnston Gate walk straight ahead to the granite University Hall (7) and the statue of a seated John Harvard. The hall was designed by Charles Bulfinch and erected in 1815. It is now used for office space. The statue was modeled by Daniel Chester French in 1884. The inscription reads "John Harvard, Founder, 1638," hence the monument's nickname, "The statue of the three lies." First, John Harvard was not the school's founder, but a benefactor. Second, the school was chartered in 1636. Third, this is not John Harvard's likeness, but rather that of a student model.

Walk around University Hall to the New Yard or

Tercentenary Theater (8). The outdoor "theater" was created for the University's 300th anniversary, in 1936, by removing older buildings and erecting Widener Library at one end of the yard and Memorial Church on the other. Commencement takes place here the first Thursday of each June amid much pomp and circumstance. The University's president and Board of Overseers sit in front of Memorial Church, facing the theater and the masses of graduates and families assembled.

The Georgian Revival Memorial Church (9) was completed in 1932. Marble tablets inscribed with the names of Harvard graduates who died in service during 20th-century wars cover the interior walls.

Visit Widener Library (10). It is dedicated as a memorial to Harry Elkins Widener (class of 1907) who perished on the *Titanic* in 1912. A beautifully paneled Memorial Room in the library displays his portrait and contains his rare book collection. The library also has an outstanding collection of over three million volumes. Of interest to the visitor may be a series of models of Harvard Square that reflects its growth through the centuries. Adjoining Widener are Pusey Library, containing archives, maps, and a permanent exhibit on alumnus Theodore Roosevelt, and Houghton Library, which includes memorabilia and furniture once owned by Emily Dickinson.

Leave Widener Library through its front door, and Sever Hall will be on the right. A Richardsonian Romanesque masterpiece by H. H. Richardson, it was built in 1880. Go to the right, walk past Emerson Hall (1905) and leave the yard at Quincy Street, which is lined by a series of the university's art museums (617-495-9400, www.artmuseums@harvard.edu). From right to left:

The statue of John Harvard overlooks Harvard Yard

Carpenter Center for the Visual Arts, designed in 1963 by LeCorbusier (11); the Busch-Reisinger Museum, built in 1991 and housing Northern European Art (12); Fogg Art Museum, built in 1927 and housing Western art from medieval times to the present (13); and the Arthur M. Sackler Museum, completed in 1985 and housing Ancient, Asian, Islamic, and Indian art (14).

Continue to walk down Quincy Street. Cross Cambridge Street to the Harvard School of Design, in Gund Hall (1972) and then cross Quincy Street to the Victorian High Gothic–style Memorial Hall (15). Built in 1878 to memorialize all Harvard students who died in the Civil War, Memorial Hall today contains the freshman dining hall, student union, and Sanders Theater. The hall is embellished with stained glass windows by Tiffany and by John LaFarge. Note the bell tower, recently restored after a long absence following a fire in the 1950s.

Option A: The Harvard Museum of Natural History, at 26 Oxford Street, presents the university's vast collections in the fields of natural and cultural history, archaeology and ethnology, comparative zoology, mineralogy, and geology. From Memorial Hall walk down Oxford Street; the Museum will be on the right (617-495-3045, www.hmnh.harvard.edu).

Option B: The Semitic Museum is in back of the Natural History Museum at 6 Divinity Avenue. Its collections focus on the ancient art of Mesopotamia, Egypt, and Cyprus (617-495-4631).

Walk to the front entrance of the Science Center (1972), turn left, and reenter the Old Yard. To the right you will see Holden Chapel (16), built in 1744, an exceptionally fine Georgian building. The chapel is flanked by Stoughton Hall (1805) on the right and Hollis Hall (1763) on the left. Note the replica of the original college pump just outside Hollis.

Make a right, walk between Massachusetts and Harvard Halls, and leave the Yard through Johnston Gate (6). Cross Massachusetts Avenue to the First Parish Church (17). An early American example of Gothic Revival, the church was built in 1833 with plans by Isaiah Rogers. Walk by the Old Burying Ground (18), which dates from 1635. It is the final resting place for colonial settlers, Revolutionary War veterans, and several Harvard presidents.

Next is Christ Church (19). An Episcopal parish, the present church was designed and built in 1759 by Peter Harrison, who is known as "America's first architect." Note the bullet hole in the narthex wall, on the right as you enter, made by a shot fired during the American Revolution. George Washington worshiped here in 1775 and sat in pew number 93 (617-876-0200).

As you exit through the doors of Christ Church look

directly ahead across Garden Street to Cambridge Common. During the American Revolution the Common was the training ground and camp for patriot troops. A newer monument on the Common commemorates the victims of the Irish Famine.

Turn left onto Garden Street and then left again onto Appian Way. Radcliffe Yard (20) will be on your right. Founded in 1879, Radcliffe and Harvard merged in 1965 to form one coeducational school. Visit Radcliffe Yard to see its significant Colonial Revival architecture.

Proceed to Brattle Street, known in the 18th century as Tory Row because of the Loyalist sympathies of its residents.

Option C: Two sites associated with Longfellow's poem "The Village Blacksmith" are on Brattle Street. To see them, make a left and stop at Blacksmith Dexter Pratt's house (now a restaurant) at number 57. A few steps farther on, near the corner of Story Street, a stone marker spots where the spreading chestnut tree described in Longfellow's poem once stood.

> *Under a spreading chestnut tree*
> *The village smithy stands;*
> *The smith, a mighty man is he,*
> *With large and sinewy hands;*
> *And the muscles of his brawny arms*
> *are strong as iron bands.*

Cross Story Street and walk just a few steps further to Brattle House (1727) at number 42. William Brattle was a physician, lawyer, preacher, and officer in the king's army—a loyalist living, appropriately, on Tory Row. Brattle House is now the Cambridge Center for Adult Education. Retrace your steps on Brattle Street.

The Henry Vassal House will be on your left just before Hawthorne Street. The house's chimney dates to the mid-1600s and stands eight feet square. Continue on Brattle Street one more block. The Longfellow National Historic Site (21) will be on the right. Built in 1759, the house later served as George Washington's headquarters. Henry Wadsworth Longfellow lived here from 1837 to 1882, and it was here he wrote some of his best loved poems, including *Evangeline* and *Hiawatha*. The house contains Longfellow's furniture, books, and memorabilia (617-876-4491, www.nps.gov/long).

Option D: The Cambridge Historical Society is in the Hooper-Lee-Nichols House (1688) at 159 Brattle Street (617-547-4252).

When leaving the Longfellow House walk straight ahead, through Longfellow Park, to the banks of the Charles River. Turn left and walk along the river (22). The Episcopal Monastery of St. Mary and St. John (23) will be on the left. Designed by American medievalist Ralph Adams Cram, the monastery's church is an outstanding example of Romanesque Revival architecture and has a beautiful, serene interior.

The John F. Kennedy Park and Harvard's John F. Kennedy School of Government (24) will be on the left as you continue along the Charles. After crossing John F. Kennedy Street you will be surrounded by Harvard once again. The Weld Boat House is on the right; the Graduate School of Business is across the river. Many of Harvard's undergraduate houses are on the left. Georgian Revival in style, most were built in the 1930s and named for university presidents: Kirkland, Eliot, Winthrop, Lowell, Quincy, and others. Walk down Plympton Street to Mount Auburn Street. The Dutch

Revival building with the round tower entrance is The Castle (25), which was built in 1909 for the Harvard *Lampoon*. First published in 1876, the *Lampoon* is this country's oldest humor magazine. Harvard students publish five editions annually. Turn left onto Mount Auburn Street and right onto Holyoke Street. The Hasty Pudding Club (26) will be on your right at number 10. Founded in 1844, the Hasty Pudding is the oldest theatrical organization in the United States and the third oldest in the world. The theater itself dates to 1889. Presented by Harvard undergraduate men, performances may best be described as "zany" (617-495-5205, www.hastypudding.org).

Walk to the end of Holyoke Street. Wadsworth House will be ahead and Harvard Square on the left.

II. Massachusetts:
More Cities and Towns

6 · Lexington

Directions: *By car:* Take MA 2 west to exit 54, Waltham Street. Take a right off the exit and follow the road to Lexington Center. Or, from MA 128, take exit 31A, MA 4 and MA 225, to Lexington. *By public transportation:* Take the T Red Line to Alewife and then take MBTA bus 62 or bus 76 to Lexington Center (1-800-392-6100, www.mbta.com).

Begin your walk at what is undoubtedly Lexington's best-known site: the statue of the Minuteman (1) at the tip of the town common, which is also known as the Battle Green. Modeled by Henry H. Kitson and dedicated in 1900, the bronze statue stands on a mound of fieldstones. The statue represents Capt. John Parker. Facing British troops on this very spot on April 19, 1775, Parker addressed his minutemen saying, "Stand your ground; Don't fire unless fired upon. But if they mean to have a war, let it begin here." (A photo of the statue is on this book's cover.)

Walk along the green parallel to Massachusetts Avenue to the Revolutionary War Monument (2). Dedicated on July 4, 1799, the monument stands in front of the final resting place of the eight minutemen killed here that fateful day in April 1775. This is believed to be the first war memorial dedicated to non-officers anywhere.

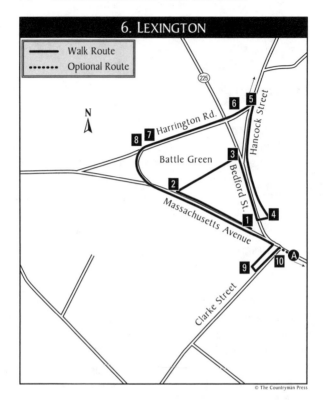

6. LEXINGTON

— Walk Route
······· Optional Route

225

Hancock Street

Harrington Rd.

Battle Green

Bedford St.

Massachusetts Avenue

Clarke Street

© The Countryman Press

Walk straight across the green to the boulder (3) on the opposite side, at Bedford Street. You are walking along the battleline that divided British and American forces before the initial skirmish of the Revolution. Known as the Parker Boulder, it is inscribed with the captain's most famous words.

Cross Bedford Street to Buckman Tavern (4). It was here that Captain Parker and many of his minutemen awaited word that the British were coming. Summoned by the sound of bells, Parker and his men assembled along the line you just walked on the green. The oldest parts of the tavern date to the 1690s. Restored to its 1775 appearance, Buckman's Tavern is open to visitors by the Lexington Historical Society (781-862-5598, www.lexingtonhistory.org/buckman).

When you leave Buckman Tavern turn right onto Bedford Street and then bear right onto Hancock Street. Walk down Hancock Street less than a third of a mile to the Hancock-Clarke House (5). A parsonage, the house is named for two men whose combined ministries in Lexington spanned more than a century: Rev. John Hancock (1698–1752) and Rev. Jonas Clarke (1755-1805). Both Samuel Adams and John Hancock (a grandson of the house's builder and the first signer of the Declaration of Independence) were guests here on April 19, 1775. Both Paul Revere and John Dawes stopped here en route to Concord, warning Adams and Hancock that the British were coming. The house is opened to the public by the Lexington Historical Society. On display are Revolutionary War artifacts, including the drum used to rally the minutemen to arms on April 19, 1775 (781-862-1703, www.lexingtonhistory.org/hancockclarke).

The Antique Fire Equipment Museum is in the barn behind the house. A treasure trove of firefighting memorabilia, the collection includes an 1857 Hunneman hand-pumper, a 1911 LaFrance firetruck, other equipment, and uniforms, photos, and documents. This is another Lexington Historical Society site (781-862-1703, www.lexintonhistory.org/museum).

Retrace your steps down Hancock Street and turn right onto Harrington Road. Note the Masonic Temple (6) on the right just before Bedford Street. Built in

1839, this was the first state normal school in America before it became a Masonic Temple.

Continue to walk down Harrington Road. The First Parish Church (7) will be on the right. The church was built in 1847 and is the fourth building to serve the parish. The first three churches, built in 1692, 1713, and 1794, stood on the common.

The Old Burying Ground (8) is also on Harrington Road. The oldest gravestones are dated 1690. The Rev. John Hancock and Capt. John Parker are among those buried here.

Harrington Road ends at Massachusetts Avenue. Turn left onto Massachusetts Avenue and then right onto Clarke Street. A replica of the old belfry (9) will be on your right. The original, destroyed in 1909, was used to summon the minutemen to arms, and was also used as a fire alarm and a church bell.

Retrace your steps to the corner of Clarke Street and Massachusetts Avenue. Visit the Cary Memorial Building and Library (10). A painting entitled *The Dawn of Liberty*, portraying the Battle of Lexington, is flanked by marble statues of Samuel Adams and John Hancock.

Option A: To visit Monroe Tavern walk east on Massachusetts Avenue about 1 mile. The Tavern dates to the 1690s. After the Battle of Lexington the British used the it as a field hospital. George Washington dined here in 1789, and an on-site museum exhibits, among other memorabilia, the table he used (781-862-1703, www. lexingtonhistory.org/monroe).

7 · Concord

Directions: *By car:* Take MA 2 west to Concord. A more scenic route is MA 2A, which passes though Minuteman National Historic Park between Lexington and Concord. *By public transportation:* Take the MBTA Commuter Rail to Concord (1-800-392-6100, www.mbta.com) or Yankee Bus Lines (1-800-942-8890).

Founded in 1635, this was the first inland Puritan settlement. At first known as Musketaquid, the name Concord was later adopted, reflecting the peaceful coexistence between the local Indians and the English settlers. Concord is best-known for the "shot heard 'round the world" and the beginning of the American Revolution on April 19, 1775. In the 19th century the town became a haven for literati, philosophers, and artists, among them Louisa May Alcott, Ralph Waldo Emerson, Nathaniel Hawthorne, Henry David Thoreau, and sculptor Daniel Chester French. Another Concord resident, Ephraim Bull, grew the first Concord grapes in 1850.

The hub of Concord is Monument Square (1), where many of the town's roads begin. At the foot of Main Street, on the square, a marker commemorates Jethro's Tree (2) and the purchase that took place near it:

Near this spot stood the ancient oak known as Jethro's Tree beneath which Major Simon Willard

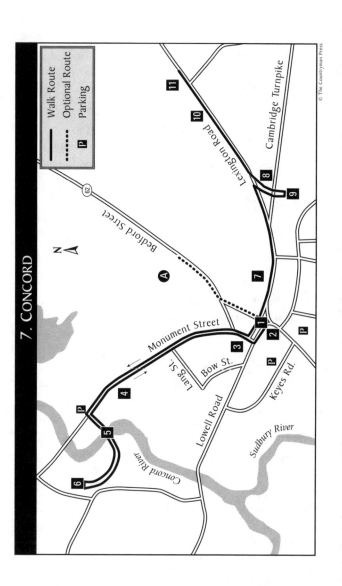

7. CONCORD

Walk Route ——
Optional Route ·····
Parking P

Bedford Street
62
Monument Street
Lowell Road
Lang St.
Bow St.
Keyes Rd.
Sudbury River
Concord River
Lexington Road
Cambridge Turnpike

N

A

© The Countryman Press

and his associates bought from the Indians the "six myles of land square" ordered by the General Court for the Plantation of Concord. September 6, 1635

Just a few steps away, the granite obelisk (1867) in the center of the square is a memorial to the Concord men killed in the Civil War and subsequent conflicts. The Colonial Inn (3) stands at the head of the square. It is not one but three buildings, the oldest of which dates to 1770. As you face the inn the wing you see on the right was once occupied by Henry David Thoreau and his family. Walk down the street to the right, Monument Street. You are walking in the footsteps of British troops who marched here on their way to the Old North Bridge. The Old Manse (4) will be on the left. The house was built in 1770 for Rev. William Emerson. His grandson Ralph Waldo Emerson lived here, too, and was inspired to write "Mosses from an Old Manse." The Old Manse is opened to the public by the Trustees for Reservations (978-369-3909, www.thetrustees.org).

The Old North Bridge (5) is just beyond the Old Manse. The statue of the Concord Minuteman was modeled by Daniel Chester French, whose most famous work is the statue of Abraham Lincoln at the Lincoln Memorial. Chiseled into the granite base of the Concord statue are Emerson's famous lines:

> *By the rude bridge that arched the flood,*
> *Their flag to April's breeze unfurled,*
> *Here once the embattled farmers stood,*
> *And fired the shot heard round the world.*

Walk over the North Bridge and follow the path through open fields and gardens to the North Bridge Visitor Center (6). In a sizable house built for a minuteman

North Bridge

descendant in 1911, the center offers an orientation film, exhibits and dioramas of the battlesite, and a shop (978-369-6993, www.nps.gov/mima).

After visiting North Bridge return to Monument Square.

Option A: To visit Sleepy Hollow Cemetery turn left onto Bedford Street (MA 62) before reaching the square. The cemetery contains the graves of Ralph Waldo Emerson, Henry David Thoreau, Nathaniel Hawthorne, Louisa May Alcott, Daniel Chester French, and many other notables.

At the end of Monument Street, at Monument Square, make an immediate left onto Lexington Road. The Concord Art Association (7) is at number 37. Note the Wright Tavern across the street. The tavern was the headquarters for British officers when they marched into Concord. Not opened to the public, Wright's Tavern is now an office building.

There is a fork in the road where Cambridge Turnpike begins. The Concord Museum (8) is at the fork. The museum contains a remarkable display of items relating to Concord's history as both a crucial site in the American Revolution and a center for 19th-century literati. You may see artifacts from the Revolution (including Paul Revere's famed lantern), Thoreau memorabilia (including the bed, desk, and chair he used at Walden Pond), Ralph Waldo Emerson's complete study, and rooms illustrating three hundred years of American decorative arts (978-369-9609, www.concordmuseum. org).

Just across Cambridge Turnpike is the Emerson House (9), the poet and essayist's home begining in 1835 and the place he died in 1882. The house is opened to visitors (978-369-2236).

Return to Lexington Road and resume your trek east. The next stop is Louis May Alcott's Orchard House (10). The author lived here for twenty years, and it was here that she penned *Little Women*. It is opened to the public (978-369-4118, www. louisamayalcott.org).

The Wayside (Home of Authors) (11) is just a few steps beyond Orchard House. The oldest parts of the building date to the 18th century and was home to a Concord Minuteman. Bronson Alcott named the house Hillside. It was Louisa May Alcott's childhood home and the setting for *Little Women*. Later Nathaniel Hawthorne acquired the house and renamed it. Margaret Sidney, children's book author, lived here and preserved the house for future generations. It is the only National Historic Landmark in which three literary authors have lived, and a part of Minute Man National Historic Park (978-369-6975, www.nps.gov/mima/wayside).

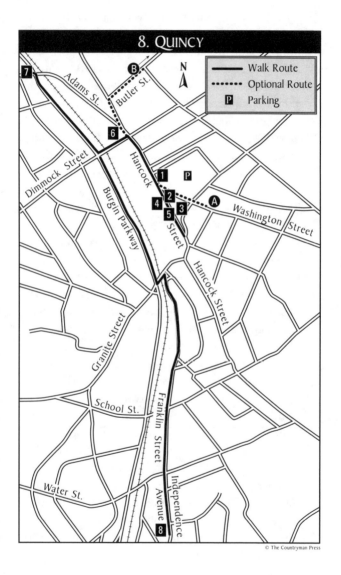

8. QUINCY

N

— Walk Route
····· Optional Route
P Parking

Adams St.
Butler St.
B
Dimmock Street
Hancock
Burgin parkway
Hancock Street
1
P
4 2
5 3
A Washington Street
6
7
Granite Street
School St.
Franklin Street
Water St.
Independence Avenue
8

© The Countryman Press

8 · Quincy

Directions: *By car:* Take I-93 south to exit 7, a left-hand exit signed for MA 3 south. Take MA 3 to exit 18, which will be the first exit on the right and is signed "Washington St./Quincy Adams T Station/Quincy Center." After exiting, bear left to Burgin Parkway/Quincy Center. *By public transportation:* Take the T Red Line to Quincy Center. Walk across Constitution Common to Hancock Street and the National Park Service's Visitor Center.

Quincy, first settled in 1625, was originally known as Mount Wollaston and later as Merry Mount. In 1792 the town was incorporated and named to honor a local resident, Col. John Quincy. Known as the City of Presidents—both John Adams and John Quincy Adams were born and buried here—the town has long been famous for its granite quarries and shipbuilding yards. There are many Quincy granite buildings on this tour.

Begin at the Adams National Historic Park Visitor Center (1), in the Presidents Place Galleria at 1250 Hancock Street. Three sites on this walking tour are a part of the park: Old House, the United First Parish Church, and the birthplaces of John and John Quincy Adams. If you plan to enter these sites be sure to buy your tickets at the visitors center. Also, keep in mind that the admission fee includes complimentary shuttle service among the park service sites, should you decide to ride as an alternative on your walking tour (617-770-1175, www.nps.gov/adam).

When you leave the visitors center turn left onto Hancock Street. Cross Washington Street. The statue of Abigail Adams and her son John Quincy Adams (2) stands on the site of the Third (Hancock) Meeting House (1732). The artist was Lloyd Lillie, and the monument was dedicated by the Quincy Partnership in 1997. Note that the First Lady is depicted looking across the street to her husband in the distance.

Next visit the United First Parish Church (3), also known as the Stone Temple and the Church of the Presidents. Built in 1828 of Quincy granite, the Greek Revival church is the work of architect Alexander Parris. Note the massive columns on the portico. Each is twenty-five feet high and weighs twenty-five tons. A plaque next to the main door reads:

Within this church are the
tombs of two
Presidents of the United States
and their wives
John Adams — Second President 1735–1826
Abigail Adams 1744–1818
Their son
John Quincy Adams — Sixth President 1767–1848
Louisa Catherine Adams 1775–1852

The tombs are in the church's crypt. An interesting aside: The only other American president buried in a church is Woodrow Wilson, whose remains are interred in Washington's National Cathedral.

Option A: The Thomas Crane Memorial Public

Library is one block from the church and is a superb example of Richardsonian Romanesque architecture. Walk down Washington Street and the library will be on the left. Thomas Crane was a descendant of Henry C. Crane, a founder of Dorchester, Massachusetts, in 1642. His formal education was limited. However, he was a master stonecutter and a good businessman, and he amassed a fortune in the granite industry. Built in 1882, the library is his memorial. Henry Hobson Richardson developed his own form of Romanesque Revival architecture; this is thought to be one of his finest works. The exterior of the library is intact; the interior of the Richardson Building (the wing to your left) has been beautifully preserved. Its carved woodwork and LaFarge stained-glass windows are particularly noteworthy (617-376-1300).

Next door to the library is the Bethany Congregational Church. Founded in 1832, the present Gothic Revival church, built in 1928, is the third to serve the congregation. Note the four gargoyles jutting from the corners of the belfry.

Directly across Hancock Street, facing the Stone Temple, you'll see Quincy's Old City Hall (4). Constructed from Quincy granite in the Greek Revival style, it dates to 1844. It was designed by Solomon Willard, whose most notable work is the Bunker Hill Monument—another Quincy granite structure.

Old City Hall is flanked on one side by Constitution Common and on the other by the Hancock Cemetery (5). The Cemetery dates to 1640 and is named for the Rev. John Hancock, the fifth minister of the Stone Temple and the father of the first signer of the Declaration of Independence. Walk through the cemetery and note the names, epitaphs, and the stonecutters' art.

Turn left out of the cemetery gate and retrace your steps down Hancock Street, passing the visitors center. On the right is the classical revival Masonic Temple. Another Quincy granite structure, its facade is embellished with Masonic symbols. The temple was built in 1926.

On the left you'll see the Quincy Historical Society (6) at the corner of Hancock and Dimmock Streets. A plaque informs the visitor:

> On this spot
> Stood the dwelling
> Wherein was born
> John Hancock
> President of the Congress
> of the United States
> XII January MDCCXXXVII

The granite and brownstone Victorian High Gothic building you see today was the Adams Academy (1872–1908), a boys' preparatory school built with funds from John Adams' estate. Visit the museum, library, and shop. The wonderful, dedicated staff are eager to share Quincy's long and diverse heritage (617-773-1144, www.ci.quincy.ma.us, click on "events and tourism").

Option B: Walk down Hancock Street to Butler Road and the Quincy Homestead. The land was granted in 1635; the Georgian mansion built in the mid-18th century. It was home to four generations of the Quincy family. John Hancock's wife, Dorothy Quincy, lived here. Independently owned and operated, the Homestead and its formal gardens are open to visitors (617-472-5117).

John Quincy Adams birthplace

From the front door of the historical society turn right at the corner onto Dimmock Steet. Then turn right at Burgin Parkway and walk along the garden path to Adams Street. The Old House (7), part of the Adams National Historic Park, will be kitty-corner on your left. It was built in 1731 and was later home to four generations of the Adams family (1788–1927). Both John and John Quincy Adams lived here with their first ladies. The house has nearly 80,000 artifacts relating to the family. After touring the house be sure to visit the carriage house (1873), the extensive formal gardens, and the family's orchard.

The next and final stop on the tour will be the Adams presidential birthplaces, also a part of the Adams National Historic Park. Ticket holders may use the park's trolley service from the Old House to the birthplaces. The distance between the two sites is 1½ miles. To walk to the birthplaces make a left at the front gate of the Old House. The next corner is Burgin Parkway. Turn right onto the parkway. Then turn left onto Granite

Street and right onto Franklin Street. (At the corner of Franklin and School Streets note the statue of the Scottish poet Robert Burns, who "penned an ode to Washington.") Use caution when crossing the busy intersection at Franklin and Water Streets. Franklin becomes Independence Avenue. The birthplaces are at number 133 and 141 Independence Avenue (8).

John Adams, second president of the United States, was born in 1735 in the 1681 saltbox farmhouse. His son, John Quincy Adams, our sixth president, was born in 1767 in the neighboring 1716 farmhouse. In addition to being the birthplaces of two presidents, the site is, in a sense, the birthplace of the U.S. Constitution. The Massachusetts State Constitution, on which the federal consitution is modeled, was written here. Tours of the houses are given by National Park Service guides. Tickets must be purchased at the visitors center. After seeing the sites return to the visitors center by trolley or by foot. If walking, retrace your steps down Independence Avenue / Franklin Street. Turn left onto Granite Street and right onto Burgin Parkway. Walk through the Quincy Center T station and Constitution Park to Hancock Street and the visitors center.

9 · Cohasset

Directions: *By car:* Take MA 3 south to exit 14. Take MA 228 north to Cohasset. Make a left onto Sohier Street to the town common. At the time of writing there is no public transportation. There are, however, plans to extend the MBTA Commuter Rail system to Cohasset. Contact the MBTA for an update (1-800-392-6100, www.mbta.com).

Captain John Smith is closely associated with Cohasset. Once the leader of the English colony of Jamestown, Virginia, he later explored the East Coast from Penobscot Bay in Maine to Cape Cod, naming the entire area New England. Smith is believed to be the first European to set foot in Cohasset, in 1614, where he "found the people in those parts very kinde." The name Cohasset derives from the Indian *quonahasset* meaning "a long, rocky place." The area was settled in 1647, and the town incorporated in 1770. Fishing, farming, and boat-building were the local economic mainstays through the early 20th century. Cohasset is now a Boston suburb and a very popular summer destination.

Begin at Cohasset Common (1), a broad expanse of lawn dotted with tall, old trees and surrounded by 18th- and 19th-century houses and other buildings. The First Parish Unitarian Meeting House stands in the

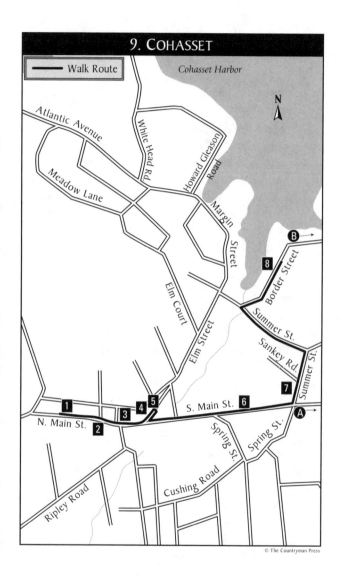

9. COHASSET

Walk Route

Cohasset Harbor

N

Atlantic Avenue

Meadow Lane

White Head Rd.

Howard Gleason Road

Margin Street

Elm Court

Elm Street

Border Street

8

B

Summer St.

Sankey Rd.

7

Summer St.

A

1

2

N. Main St.

3 **4** **5**

S. Main St. **6**

Spring St.

Spring St.

Cushing Road

Ripley Road

© The Countryman Press

center of the common. Built in 1747, it has a simple, elegant exterior and a tall, slender spire.

Walk past the pond and along Main Street. On your right, across from the common, you'll see the Elisha Doane House (2). It was built in 1760 and today is the Cohasset Community center.

As you continue along Main Street, St. Stephen's Church (Episcopal) (3) will be on your left, dramatically perched on top of a rocky hill overlooking the town. Climb the steps to get a closer look at the church. Perpendicular Gothic in style, it was built of granite in 1900 according to plans drawn by the firm of Cram, Goodhue, and Ferguson. The adjoining structures are half timber and plaster. The massive bell tower houses a fifty-one-bell carillon. The interior is lit by exceptional stained-glass windows.

Resume your walk on South Main Street and turn left onto Elm Street. Two museums of the Cohasset Historical Society will be on your left. The Captain John Wilson House (4), built in 1810, is a modest but handsome dwelling filled with period furnishings and decorative arts. The Maritime Museum (5) is next door at 4 Elm Street. Built in the 18th century as the Bates Ship Chandlery, this commercial building was moved here from Bate's Wharf in Cohasset Harbor in 1957. The museum contains not only nautical memorabilia and ship models, but also a collection of Indian artifacts, objects related to Cohasset's history, and an exhibit recounting the building of Minot's Ledge Lighthouse, featured later on the tour (781-383-1434).

Return to South Main Street and continue to walk east. The Red Lion Inn will be on the right. Initially built as a house in 1704, it was opened to the public for food and lodging two generations later.

Walk a few steps farther along South Main Street. The Paul Pratt Memorial Library (6) will be across the street on the left. The central portion of this Colonial Revival building was completed in 1904; wings have been added since. Enter the library at the columned portico. Under the cupola there is a circular, wood-paneled room with a domed ceiling. Just under the dome the walls are covered with a series of four murals depicting chapters in Cohasset's history.

Return to South Main Street, turn left, and walk to Summer Street.

Option A: Just beyond Summer Street, you'll see the Joshua Bates House on the right at number 179 South Main Street. The house was built in 1695 and remains a private residence.

Make a left on Summer Street. The Caleb Lothrop House (7) will be on the left at number 14. This is a brick-end, Federal house built in 1821. It is the Cohasset Historical Society's headquarters, library, and archive, and is opened by appointment (781-343-1434).

Summer Street will bear to the left and will bring you to the foot of Border Street. Turn right onto Border Street. Cohasset Harbor will be on the left. At the pavilion (8) a plaque, placed here in 1914, reads:

> To commemorate the
> Discovery of Cohasset
> in 1614 by
> Captain John Smith
> President of Virginia and
> Admiral of New England

Option B: In the pavilion there is a map of the Captain's Walk, which will lead you along the shore, visiting many 18th- and 19th-century historical sites along the way.

To get a look at Minot's Ledge Lighthouse, walk past the Atlantica Restaurant and look across the harbor beyond the moored yachts to the lighthouse, two-and-a-half miles from land. Cohasset Harbor is filled with rocky ledges and was the scene of many tragic shipwrecks. The lighthouse, built in 1860, flashes a signal to vessels: 1–4–3 ("I love you").

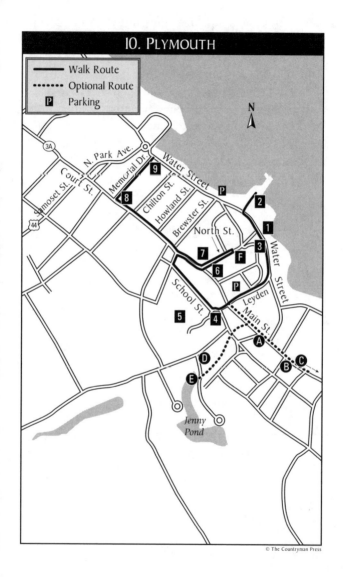

10. PLYMOUTH

Walk Route
Optional Route
P Parking

N

3A

N. Park Ave.
Water Street

Court St.
Memorial Dr.
9

Samoset St.
44
8

Chilton St.
Howland St.
Brewster St.
P

2

North St.
1

7
F
3

6
Water Street

P

School St.
Leyden

5
4
Main St.
A

D
B
C

E

Jenny
Pond

© The Countryman Press

IO · Plymouth

Directions: *By car:* Take MA 3 south to exit 6A. *By public transportation:* The Plymouth & Brockton Street Railway Co. provides bus service (617-773-9401, www.p-b.com).

In 1620 the *Mayflower* embarked from Plymouth, England. The Pilgrims named their new settlement after the English city. The tour begins at Plymouth's most fabled site: Plymouth Rock (1). When the Pilgrims arrived here on December 26, 1620, they moored the *Mayflower* offshore, rowed in, and set foot on land at this very spot. In 1741 an older citizen of the town, Thomas Faunce, recounted the story he was told as a boy, identifying the rock. A portion of the rock was broken off and displayed elsewhere in town in 1775; in 1889 the rock was put together again and cemented. In 1921, three hundred years after the Pilgrims landed, the National Society of the Colonial Dames of America built the Classical Revival granite temple that enshrines and protects Plymouth Rock.

A few steps down Water Street is the *Mayflower II* (2). Built in England in 1955, this full-scale replica of the original retraced the voyage across the Atlantic and is now permanently docked. The ship is 106 feet long and was constructed in Brixham, England, of oak. A goodwill gift from Great Britain, *Mayflower II* is now a part of Plimoth

Plantation. Costumed interpreters on board greet and guide visitors (508-746-1622, www.plimoth.org).

Across Water Street, the Pilgrim Mother statue, designed by McKim, Mead, and White in 1921, was placed here by the National Society of the Daughters of the American Revolution.

Retrace your steps up Water Street. Cole's Hill (3) is on the right, just beyond North Street. Many Pilgrims did not survive their first winter in the New World. Cole's Hill (formerly an Indian cornfield) was their burial ground. Note the granite sarcophagus (1920) that contains the exhumed remains. A statue of Massasoit stands nearby. Massasoit, the sachem of the Wampanoag tribe, was a good friend to the English settlers. The statue was modeled by Cyrus Dallin in 1921.

Turn right onto Leyden Street and begin your ascent up the hill. This street, Plymouth's first, was the site of the original foundation. Many of the Pilgrims had lived in Leyden, Holland, before setting sail for America. Note the Town Brook, which supplied fresh water to the early settlers. The paths through this park, known as Brewster Gardens, will lead up the hill to Town Square (4). The Pilgrim Maiden statue is en route.

Option A: Howland House, at 33 Sandwich Street, was built in 1666. It is the only Pilgrim residence still standing in Plymouth. It is opened to the public by the John Howland Society and is staffed by guides dressed in period costumes (508-746-9590).

Option B: The Training Green is behind the Howland House, between Sandwich and Pleasant Streets. In the 19th century it was landscaped by Frederick Law Olmsted.

Option C: Walk down Sandwich Street about ¼

Mayflower II

mile to the Harlow Old Fort House, built in 1677 with timbers from the First Fort. Costumed guides welcome visitors and demonstrate everyday chores performed in colonial homes. The house is owned by the Plymouth Antiquarian Society (508-746-0012).

Continue uphill to Town Square, the heart of the colonial town. The 1749 Court House and Museum will be on your left. This, the oldest wooden courthouse in the nation, is a museum with exhibits on Plymouth's early history (508-830-4075).

Note the two churches in Town Square. Both are descendants of the original Pilgrim congregation, which split in 1801 over a matter of doctrine—Trinitarians versus Unitarians. The Unitarians retained the title First Parish Church and occupy the impressive Romanesque Revival stone church at the head of the square. The Trinitarians now form the Church of the Pilgrims and worship in the white clapboard Palladian church to your right.

Option D: The path along the Town Brook will lead you to the Sparrow House. Built in 1640 for Richard Sparrow and his family, this is the oldest house in Plymouth. The Pottery Gallery is adjacent. Both house and gallery welcome visitors (508-747-1240, www.sparrowhouse.com).

Option E: The path in Brewster Gardens ultimately leads to Jenny Pond. John Jenny's Grist Mill, constructed in 1636, has been re-created at 6 Spring Lane. A museum, gift shop, and ice cream shop welcome visitors (508-747-4544).

From Town Square walk along School Street and visit Burial Hill (5). The Pilgrims built many of their first community structures here: the First Fort, Watchtower, Old Powder House, and Meetinghouse. The earliest graves date to the 17th century. Burial Hill has panoramic views of the town, harbor, and surrounding countryside. Look directly north and you will see the towering National Monument to the Forefathers. Eighty-one feet tall, this is the world's largest freestanding granite statue. Dedicated in 1889 and modeled by Hammet Billings, the monument portrays the Pilgrims' virtues: morality, liberty, education, and law. The massive statue on top of the monument represents Faith. With right hand upraised, she is reminiscent of the Statue of Liberty. Should you wish to visit the monument later, it is located at the intersection of Samoset (US 44) and Allerton Streets.

Begin descending the hill. The next stop is the Spooner House (6), at 27 North Street near Main Street. The 1749 house was home to the Spooner family for over two hundred years and features period furnishings from the 18th to 20th centuries, antique toys, and a secret garden. It is opened to the public by the Plymouth Antiquarian Society (508-746-0012).

The Taylor Trask Museum, at 35 North Street and built in 1829, is open by appointment (508-747-0686).

Next is the Mayflower Society House Museum (7) at 4 Winslow Street. The oldest part of the house dates to 1754 and was built for Edward Winslow, a descendant of Pilgrims and of Massachusetts Governor Edward Winslow. The house was later bought by Dr. Charles Jackson who, with his assistant, Dr. William Morton, first used ether in medicine in 1842. Dr. Jackson's sister Lydia married Ralph Waldo Emerson in this house in 1835. In 1898 the house was sold and expanded, its new wings incorporating Colonial Revival details. Outstanding features include nine rooms furnished with period pieces, an elegant "flying stairway," and flower gardens (508-746-2590).

Option F: The Plymouth National Wax Museum (16 Carver Street) exhibits the Pilgrims' story with 180 lifesize wax figures in 24 dioramas (508-746-6468).

Retrace your steps to Main Street and turn right. Main Street becomes Court Street. Just beyond Clinton Street is Pilgrim Hall Museum (8), at 75 Court Street. Founded in 1824, it is believed to be the oldest continuously operating public museum in America. The collection concentrates on Pilgrim artifacts and memorabilia: John Alden's bible, Captain Myles Standish's sword, period furniture, household items, and weapons. The only authentic remnants of a 17th-century trans-Atlantic vessel are on display. The museum is owned and operated by the Pilgrim Society (508-746-1620, www.pilgrimhall.org).

When you leave the museum, go around the block, making a right on Court Street. Make another right on Memorial Drive, and a right on Water Street. The Hedge House Museum (9), at 126 Water Street, is the headquarters for the Plymouth Antiquarian Society. Housed in an 1809 Federal mansion, the museum exhibits period furnishings, imports from the China trade, clothing, and antique toys. Special exhibits from the Society's collection are mounted (508-746-0012).

II · Sandwich, Cape Cod

Directions: *By car:* Take MA 3 south and cross the Sagamore Bridge to Cape Cod. Take US 6, the Mid-Cape Highway, east to exit 2. At the bottom of the ramp turn left onto MA 130 north. Follow MA 130 for 2 miles. Bear right at the fork. *By public transportation:* Take a Plymouth & Brockton Street Railway bus (617-773-9401, www.p-b.com) to the rotary just before the Sagamore Bridge. Phone in advance to be met by a Sandwich Taxi (508-888-7174).

The English explorer Bartholomew Gosnold gave Cape Cod its name in 1602, referring to its "great store of codfish." The *Mayflower*'s Pilgrims set foot on Cape Cod at Provincetown before making their permanent settlement in Plymouth.

Sandwich is the oldest European settlement on the Cape. It was founded in 1637, named for Sandwich, England, and has nothing to do with the sandwich one eats. A century after this town was founded the Earl of Sandwich popularized the food item. In the 1800s the town became well known for its pressed glass, some of which you will see on the tour.

Begin at the Daniel Webster Inn (1). The earliest house on this site was built in 1692. At first a parsonage,

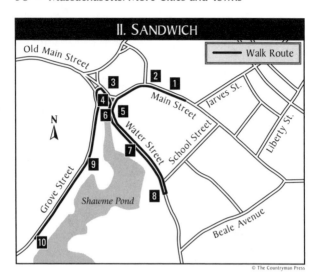

© The Countryman Press

it later became an inn known as the Fessenden Tavern. During the American Revolution the inn was a patriot headquarters. Daniel Webster, statesman and orator, had a reserved room and used it on hunting and fishing trips until 1851. The inn was renamed for Webster in 1915. Through the years it has been visited by other notables, such as Henry David Thoreau, Helen Keller, several U.S. Presidents, and more recently by the Empress of Japan. The old tavern was destroyed by fire in 1971, rebuilt, and is maintained by the Catania family, who offer good food and modern levels of comfort while being sensitive to the inn's long history and heritage (508-888-3622, www.danlwebsterinn.com).

From the door of the Daniel Webster Inn turn right onto Main Street. Yesteryear's Doll Museum (2), which exhibits antique and rare dolls, will be on the right.

Walk to the Sandwich Glass Museum and Glassworks (3) at the corner of Main Street and Topper Road. In 1825 the Boston and Sandwich Glass Company opened the town's first glassworks, which in time transformed this farming and fishing community into a large glass-manufacturing center specializing in pressed glass, a new process at that time. The museum has 14 galleries exhibiting over five thousand pieces of Sandwich glass. There is a diorama of the original glass factory, a glass furnace, and glassmaking demonstrations (508-888-0251, www.sandwichglassmuseum.org).

When you leave the museum look across Main Street to the Town Hall (4), built in 1834. The First Church of Christ (5) is on the left. Built in 1847, its elegant spire copies the works of Sir Christopher Wren, who designed so many churches in London.

Cross the street and turn left onto Water Street. The Dexter Grist Mill (6) will be on the right. There has been an operating mill on this spot since the mid-1600s. Townsfolk would bring their corn to the mill to be ground into meal. Today, the mill is open to visitors, and you may see corn ground here (508-888-5144).

Walk a few steps farther on Water Street to the Thornton Burgess Museum (7). A well-known author of children's books, Burgess was born in Sandwich in 1874. The museum displays his mementos, manuscripts, and illustrations (508-888-4668, www.thorntonburgess.org/museum).

Walk past the Shawme Pond, a favorite gathering place for ducks and other fowl. The next stop is the Hoxie House Museum (8). A dwelling built in 1653, its interior, furnished with period pieces, is open to visitors (508-888-0251).

Walk back to Town Hall, make a hairpin turn to the

CAPE COD CHAMBER OF COMMERCE

Dexter Grist Mill

left, and walk down Grove Street. The Old Town Cemetery (9) will be on the left. Its oldest tombstone is dated 1683. About half a mile further along Grove Street you will see the entrance to The Heritage Museums and Gardens (10). Several museums dot the 100-acre garden setting, which is planted with award-winning rhododendrons, daylilies, and many other flowers, shrubs, and trees, their blossoming times reflecting the seasons. The museums include: a reproduction Shaker round barn, which, surprisingly, houses one of the world's best collections of antique automobiles; the American History Museum, which has historic flags, antique toys, Indian artifacts, and memorabilia; and the Art Museum, known for its collection of American folk art. There is also a 200-year-old windmill, a hand-carved, operating carousel built in 1912, a shop, and the Carousel Cafe (508-888-3300, www.heritageplantation.org).

12 · Nantucket

Directions: *By car:* Take MA 3 south. Cross the Sagamore Bridge, and take US 6, the Mid-Cape Highway, to exit 7 (Yarmouth-Willow Street/Yarmouth Road). Take a left from the exit ramp and cross MA 28 to East Main Street. At the stop sign turn right onto Main Street and take the first left onto Pleasant Street. The South Street Dock is at the corner of Pleasant and South Streets. Take the ferry to Nantucket. *By public transportation:* Your options are to take a bus and then a ferry, or to fly. Bonanza Bus (1-800-556-3815, www.bonanzabus.com) and Plymouth & Brockton Bus (617-773-9401, www.p-b.com) both offer service to Hyannis. From there, take a ferry to Nantucket: either Hy-Line Cruises (1-800-492-8082, www.hy-linecruises.com) or the Steamship Authority (1-800-352-7144, www.islandferry.com). Cape Air Nantucket Airlines has service from Boston (1-800-352-0714, www.flycapeair.com).

Nantucket, thirty miles south of Cape Cod, is an idyllic island just fifteen miles long and six miles wide. Its name is Indian, but the meaning is unclear. The most popular translation is "far away island." The

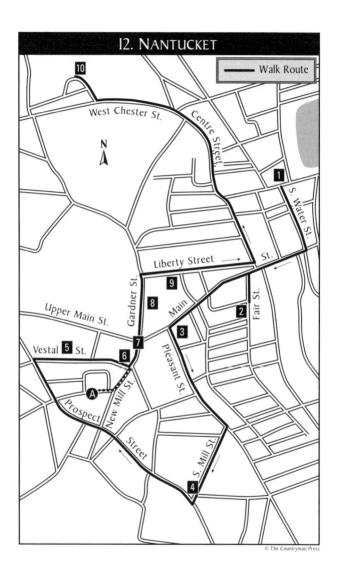

12. NANTUCKET

Walk Route

West Chester St.

Centre Street

N

10

1

S. Water St.

Liberty Street

St.

9

Gardner St.

8

Main

2

Fair St.

Upper Main St.

3

Vestal **5** St.

7

6

Pleasant St.

A

New Mill St.

Prospect

Street

S. Mill St.

4

© The Countryman Press

first European to set foot on the island was an Englishman, Bartholomew Gosnold, in 1602. The island was settled by Quakers in 1659. Fishing, trading, and shipbuilding were their first industries. In the 18th century whaling was the colonists' biggest business, and Nantucket was homeport to more than 125 whaling ships.

The Whaling Museum (1) and many of the sites on this walking tour are administered by the Nantucket Historical Association (NHA). Tickets for all their properties are on sale at the Whaling Museum (508-228-1894, www.nha.org).

Housed in a former factory where spermaceti candles were manufactured from whale oil, the Nantucket Whaling Museum exhibits memorabilia and artifacts. Its permanent collection includes a whale skeleton, ship models, an extensive scrimshaw collection, whaling tools, documents, and portraits of sea captains. Permanently mounted exhibits include the South Seas Collection, Maritime Folk Art, and Whaling, Then and Now. Artifacts from the *Essex,* the ship that inspired Herman Melville's novel *Moby Dick,* are on display.

The Peter Foulger Museum next door has objects relating to other aspects of Nantucket's history: portraits, furniture, and a collection of the world-famous Nantucket baskets.

Walk down South Water Street and turn right onto Main Street, a cobblestoned street that is undoubtedly one of the most charming in New England. Turn left onto Fair Street and visit the Quaker Meeting House (2), built in 1838. Returning to Main Street, turn left. Across the street, on the right, note the Three Bricks, three 19th-century, identical houses built for three sons of a wealthy merchant. Stop at the Hadwen House (3), number 96. Another NHA property, this Greek Revival mansion was built in 1845 for William Hadwen, whose fortune came from candlemaking.

After touring the Hadwen House turn left onto Pleasant Street and then right onto South Mill Street. Stop at the Old Mill (4). Built in 1745, this is the oldest functioning mill in America. It is the last of the four windmills that stood on this hill overlooking the town. An NHA site, the Old Mill is open to visitors, who may watch corn being ground.

When you leave the wind mill, walk down Prospect Street to Milk Street. Jog left a bit and walk down Quaker Road. Turn right onto Vestal Street. The Old Gaol (5) will be on your left. The first gaol was built here in 1696. The present Gaol, built in 1805, was last used "for purposes intended" in 1933. This is another NHA property open to visitors.

The Maria Mitchell Birthplace House (6) is at One Vestal Street. Born in 1818, she was America's first woman astronomer and in fact discovered a comet that is named for her. Her house, built in 1790, is an excellent example of a simple colonial Quaker house (508-228-2896).

Option A: Nearby, at 7 Milk Street, you may visit the Hinchman House Museum of Natural History. Affiliated with the Mitchell House, combination tickets for both properties are on sale (508-228-0898).

The Soldiers and Sailors Civil War Monument (7) stands at the corner of Milk and Maiden Streets. Cross Main Street to Gardner Street. The Fire Hose Cart House (8) is at 8 Gardner. Built in 1886, this is the last remaining 19th-century firehouse on the island. Maintained by the NHA, the house has a museum of fire-fighting equipment.

Turn right onto Liberty Street. The Macy-Christian House (9) is at number 12. The house, constructed in 1745, is furnished with 18th century antiques and later colonial revival decorative arts and is maintained by the NHA.

Turn left onto Centre Street. The Methodist and First Congregational Churches will be on the left. The tour ends on the peak of Sunset Hill at the Jethro Coffin House (10). Popularly known as the Oldest House, it dates to 1686. A saltbox, it is the only building standing on Nantucket Island since the time of the first English settlement. The house is open to visitors by the NHA.

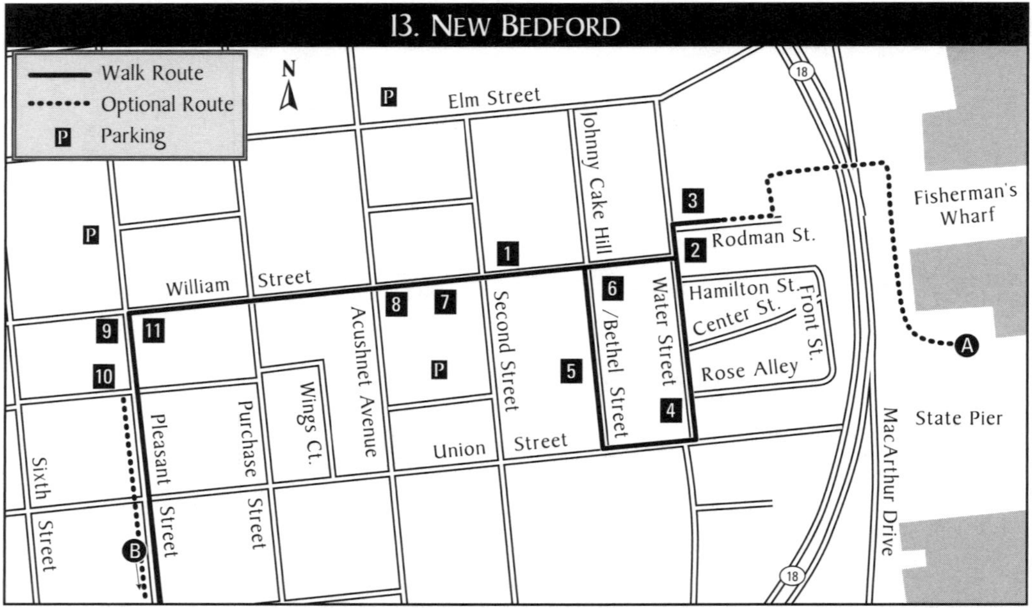

13. NEW BEDFORD

Walk Route
Optional Route
P Parking

N

Fisherman's Wharf

State Pier

MacArthur Drive

A

18

Rodman St.

Front St.
Hamilton St.
Center St.
Rose Alley

3

2

Water Street 4

Johnny Cake Hill

6 /Bethel Street

5

Elm Street

1

Second Street

Union Street

7

P

8

Acushnet Avenue

William Street

Wings Ct.

Purchase Street

11

Pleasant Street

B

9 10

Sixth Street

P

P

18

© The Countryman Press

13 · New Bedford

Directions: *By car:* From MA 128 take MA 24 south to exit 12. Take MA 140 south to I-195 east. Take exit 15 to MA 18 south. *By public transportation:* Bonanza Bus offers service to New Bedford (1-888-751-8800, www.bonanzabus.com).

This area was settled by colonists from Plymouth in 1652 and for many years was a part of the town of Dartmouth. "New" Bedford was established in 1787, its name distinguishing it from Bedford, Massachusetts. As early as the 1760s this was a whaling and shipbuilding center. By the 1820s New Bedford was one of the largest and busiest whaling ports in the world and home to ten thousand seamen. Herman Melville was one of them, and was inspired here to pen his classic *Moby Dick.* While the whaling industry is but a memory, fishing still plays a large role in this, the East Coast's largest fishing port.

Much of this walk is within New Bedford National Historic Park. Start at the park's visitors center (1) at the corner of William and North Second Streets. The center is located in a brownstone Greek Revival building that was built in 1853.

When you leave the visitors center turn left and walk down William Street. At the foot of the street you'll see

New Bedford Whaling Museum with a view of historic North Water Street

another Greek Revival building, the Double Bank Building (2). The long portico is supported by a row of eight Ionic columns. Providence architect Russell Warren designed the building to house two banks in this, New Bedford's financial district.

The Rodman Candleworks (3) is on your left. Spermaceti (whale oil) candles were made here. Built in Federal style in 1810, the stucco facade was made to resemble stone blocks.

Option A: To visit the waterfront, walk down Rodman Street to the footbridge and cross MA 18. The schooner *Ernestina* is often docked at Tonnessen Park on the banks of the Acushnet River. Originally christened the *Effie Morrissey* in Essex in 1894, the schooner later became the property of Cape Verde. A gift from the people of Cape Verde, the *Ernestina* is a National Historic Landmark and an official vessel of Massachusetts.

With your back to the door of the Double Bank Building turn left and walk along North Water Street to

Union Street. Note the sundial on the facade that faces Union Street. Clocks and chronometers were manufactured in this building for many years, which is now the Steamship Foundation's headquarters (4).

From Union Street turn right onto Johnny Cake Hill. The chapel on the left is the Seamen's Bethel (5). Built by the New Bedford Port Society in 1832, Herman Melville first visited this chapel in 1840 and later described it in *Moby Dick*. After a fire in 1866 several structural and design changes were made. Note the pulpit that resembles a ship's bow and the walls covered with numerous marble tributes to seamen. Today the New Bedford Port Society and the Seamen's Bethel continue to minister to the "sons of Neptune."

Next door to the Seamen's Bethel is the Mariner's Home. Built in 1787 as a house for William J. Rotch Jr., it was moved to its present site in 1851 and converted to a resting place for transient seamen. It is owned by the New Bedford Port Society.

Across the street is the New Bedford Whaling Museum (6). Walk to the museum's entrance (and newest wing) at the corner of Johnny Cake Hill/Bethel Street and William Street. On entering the museum you'll be greeted by the sight of the skeletal remains of a sixty-six-foot-long blue whale. Be sure to explore the museum's galleries, which contain one of the world's largest and most outstanding collections of whaling artifacts, memorabilia, and artwork: scrimshaw, paintings, prints, drawings, ship models, and documents. There is a walk-on (and hands-on) half-scale model of the whaleship *Lagoda*, and interactive exhibits on whales (508-997-0046, www.whalingmuseum.org).

From the Whaling Museum walk up to the U.S.

Custom House (7) at the corner of William and North Second Streets. Built in 1836, this is the oldest custom-house in America still in use today. The granite, Greek Revival structure was designed by Robert Mills, whose best-known work is the Washington Monument. Interestingly, Mills designed very similar customhouses for Newburyport, Massachusetts, (now a museum, see page 131) and New London, Connecticut. Compare the Doric columns here with the Ionic columns on the Double Bank Building just two blocks down William Street.

As you walk up William Street behind the Custom House you'll see the plaza dedicated to the 54th Regiment of the Massachusetts Volunteer Infantry (8), which commemorates the first African American regiment ever commissioned. The local recruiting station was on this site, and the 54th served in the Civil War. The story is retold in the film *Glory.*

Stop at the corner of William and Pleasant Streets. Across Pleasant Street to the right is the red brick and brownstone City Hall. To its left is the granite public library. Two statues stand in front of the library. *The Whaleman* (9) is on the right. It was modeled by Bela Pratt in 1913. Behind the *Whaleman* is inscribed the whaler's motto: "A dead whale or a stove boat." The back of the monument reads:

In Honor of the
Whalemen whose skill
hardihood and daring brought
fame and fortune to
New Bedford and made its name
known to every
seaport on the globe.

The statue on the left is a monument to New Bedford blacksmith Lewis Temple. Temple was a black man who invented the iron toggle harpoon tip. The statue was modeled by Jim Toatley in 1987.

Opposite the library is the New Bedford Art Museum (10) at 608 Pleasant Street. This is a newer art museum that highlights the city's collection, works by local artists, and special exhibits and educational programs (508-961-3072).

Option B: From the ending point of this tour it is a ten-minute walk to the Rotch-Jones-Duff House and Garden Museum (396 County Street). Walk along Pleasant Street to Madison Street. Make a right on Madison Street and then a left on County Street. Built in 1834 for whaling merchant William Rotch, Jr., this Greek Revival mansion has been restored and fully furnished with period pieces. Set in a full city block surrounded by gardens, the site includes a wildflower walk, formal boxwood rose parterre, and a historic wood pergola (508-997-1401; www.rjdmuseum.org).

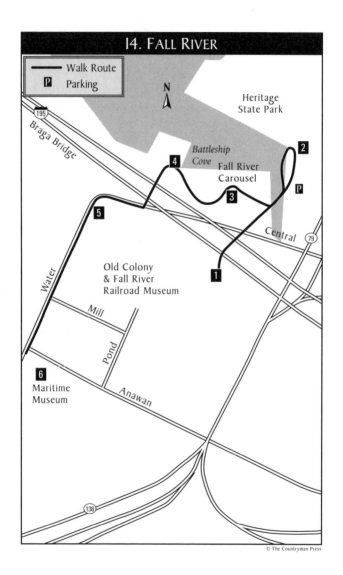

14. FALL RIVER

Walk Route
P Parking

N

I-195

Braga Bridge

Heritage
State Park

Battleship
Cove

Fall River
Carousel

4

2

P

3

Central

79

5

Old Colony
& Fall River
Railroad Museum

1

Water

Mill

Pond

Anawan

6
Maritime
Museum

138

© The Countryman Press

14 · Fall River

Directions: *By car:* From MA 128 take MA 24 south to exit 7. Take MA 79/MA 138 south to the Davol Street exit. Heritage State Park will be on the right. *By public transportation:* Take Bonanza Bus (1-888-751-8800, www.bonanza-bus.com) or Bloom Bus (1-800-323-3009, www.bloombus.com) to Fall River. The bus will let you off in front of the station on Second Street, across the street from the Lizzie Borden House. Facing the Lizzie Borden House, turn left and walk two blocks to Bedford Street. Turn left onto Bedford, which will become Central Street, which leads you to the riverfront and the beginning of this short tour, a five-minute walk.

Mention Fall River to many and their immediate recollection is of Lizzie Borden, who in 1892 "took an ax and gave her mother forty whacks." True, Lizzie may be Fall River's most famous person, but the city of "hills, mills, cobblestones and dinner pails" has a lot more to offer today's visitor.

Fall River is a loose translation of the Indian name for the site; it would more accurately be Falling Waters. The area was bought from the Indians in 1659, and the city incorporated in 1803, situated at the mouth of the

Taunton River. The water supplied power to the many mills that sprung up here in the 19th century. It is said that enough cotton cloth was made in Fall River to wrap around the world fifty times. No longer operating, many of the mills now house factory outlet shops. The tour concentrates on sites along the Taunton River.

This walk is overshadowed (literally) by a bridge. Spanning the Taunton River, the Charles W. Braga Jr. Memorial Bridge (1) was built in 1965. Begin at the foot of Central Street. The footbridge on your right leads to Fall River Heritage State Park (2). The park's visitors center has videos, photos, and exhibits illustrating Fall River's history. Climb the bell tower to get a panoramic view of the city, the river, and the surrounding countryside. The 8½-acre park has a waterfront boardwalk. Sailboats are available for rent (508-675-5759).

Retrace your steps over the footbridge. The circular pavilion encloses the Philadelphia Toboggan Company Carousel #54 (3). From its creation, in 1920, until 1986 this carousel was enjoyed by generations of families visiting Lincoln Park in Lincoln, Rhode Island. In 1991 the 48 hand-carved horses and two chariots were meticulously restored; the carousel has been here in Fall River since 1992 (508-324-4300).

You are on the shores of Battleship Cove (4), where six naval vessels are permanently docked. The largest and most noteworthy is the battleship U.S.S. *Massachusetts*. Commissioned in 1942, she is as tall as a nine-story building and as long as two football fields. You may walk Big Mamie's deck and explore the inside. Also visit the destroyer U.S.S. *Joseph P. Kennedy, Jr.*, the submarine U.S.S. *Lionfish*, the Russian missile corvette *Hid-*

densea, and two torpedo boats: PT 796 and PT 617 (1-800-533-3194 or 508-678-1100, www.battleship@battle-shipcove.com).

After visiting the battleships walk under the Braga Bridge to the corner of Central and Water Streets. The Old Colony and Fall River Railroad Museum (5) preserves and displays its collection of old railroad cars and other memorabilia (508-674-9340, www.ocandfrrail-roadmuseum.com).

Continue down Water Street. The Marine Museum (6) will be on the left. On permanent exhibit is a 28-foot-long model of the *Titanic* made for the film *A Night to Remember.* There is an extensive exhibit of artifacts from the Fall River Line, which provided luxurious, overnight transportation to and from New York City on "floating palaces" from 1847 until 1937 (508-674-3533).

Also nearby: The Fall River Historical Society, at 451 Rock Street (508-679-1071, www.lizzieborden.org).

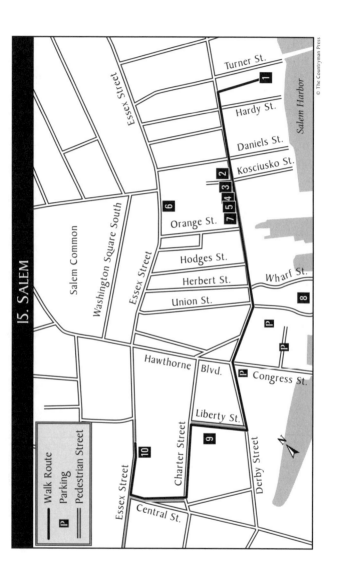

15. SALEM

Turner St.
Essex Street
1
Salem Harbor
Hardy St.
Daniels St.
Kosciusko St.
2
3
6
7 5 4
Orange St.
Hodges St.
Herbert St.
Wharf St.
Union St.
8
P
P
Hawthorne Blvd.
P Congress St.
Salem Common
Washington Square South
Essex Street
Liberty St.
9
Charter Street
Derby Street
10
Essex Street
Central St.

Walk Route
P Parking
Pedestrian Street

N

© The Countryman Press

15 · Salem

Directions: *By car:* Take MA 128 north to exit 25A (MA 114). Follow MA 114 east to Salem. *By public transportation:* Take the MBTA Commuter Rail from North Station to Salem. Or take the T Green Line to Haymarket and then MBTA bus 450 or 455 (1-800-392-6100, www.mbta.com).

Salem, the City of Peace, was founded in 1626. Before the century's end—in 1692—the village became engulfed in a series of witch trials. Later, in the 18th and 19th centuries, it was a major port and shipbuilding center. Its most famous citizen is probably Nathaniel Hawthorne, who was born here, worked in Salem's Custom House, and was inspired to write *The House of the Seven Gables, The Scarlet Letter,* and other works. The city has a remarkable architectural legacy, much of which you will see on this tour.

The Turner-Ingersoll Mansion, better known as the House of the Seven Gables, at 54 Turner Street (1), marks the starting point of the tour of historic Salem. Built in 1668, it is the oldest surviving mansion in New England. Costumed interpreters guide visitors through the house, its Colonial Revival gardens, and the transplanted Nathaniel Hawthorne birthplace. Hawthorne's writing desk and other possessions are on exhibit. A

HOUSE OF THE SEVEN GABLES HISTORIC SITE

House of the Seven Gables

garden café and a museum store are also on the site, all
of which overlook Salem Harbor (978-744-0991, www.
7gables.org).

From the House of the Seven Gables walk down
Derby Street to the Salem Maritime National Historic
Site. Tour numbers 2 through 7 are all a part of the site.

The Central Wharf Warehouse Orientation Center, at 174 Derby Street, is a good starting point. Then continue your stroll, visiting the site's buildings.

The Polish Club (2) was built in 1909 and served as a community center for Polish immigrants for half a century.

The West India Goods Store (3), built circa 1800, sold imported goods.

The Derby House (4), the oldest brick house in Salem, was built in 1762 for shipowner Elias Hasket Derby, who also gave his name to Derby Wharf.

The Hawkes House (5) was built in 1780 as a warehouse for Derby. Benjamin Hawkes bought the building and renovated it to its present appearance in 1801.

The Narbonne-Haley House (6) was built in the 1600s and has served at various times as a home and shop for a number of people.

The Custom House (1819) (7) is a Federal building. The eagle above the Palladian window identifies this as an office of the federal government. An interesting aside: Nathaniel Hawthorne worked for a time as a customs agent. It is said that here he found a patch of fabric that inspired him to write *The Scarlet Letter*.

A lighthouse (1871) sits at the end of Derby Wharf, one of over fifty wharves that jutted into Salem Harbor two hundred years ago. Central Wharf and Hatch's Wharf are also part of the Salem Maritime National Historic Site.

After visiting the site continue your walk along Derby Street. Pickering Wharf (8) will be on your left. A re-creation of an 18th-century wharf, it offers many shops and restaurants.

Turn right onto Liberty Street, a pedestrian mall. The

Old Burying Point Cemetery (9) will be on your left. A plaque here reads:

> This ground
> the first place set apart in
> Salem
> for the burial of the dead.
> And, since 1637, known as
> The Burying Point,
> contains the graves of
> Governor Bradstreet,
> Chief Justice Lynde,
> and others whose virtues,
> honors, courage, and sagacity
> have nobly illustrated
> the history of Salem.

The witch trial memorial is at the corner of Liberty and Charter Streets and commemorates the 14 women and 5 men who were executed during Salem's infamous witch hunt in 1692. One man was crushed to death under the weight of stones; the others were hanged.

Turn left onto Charter Street and then right at the pedestrian walkway at Central Street, and right again onto the Essex Street Pedestrian Mall. The Peabody Essex Museum (10) will be on your right at East India Square.

The Peabody Essex Museum, New England's third largest, is at once one of the oldest and newest museums in America. Founded in 1795 by the East India Marine Society, the museum completed a one-hundred-million-dollar building project in 2003. The collection is as varied as it is impressive, with nearly two-and-a-half million works of art. This includes the world's foremost collection of Asian export art, Asian art (including a complete Qing Dynasty house with original furnishings), American decorative arts, folk art and costumes, maritime art, and Oceanic, African, and Native American art. The museum includes 23 historic properties. Clustered near the main building are the John Ward House (a First Period dwelling from about 1684), the Georgian Crowingshield-Bentley House (c. 1727), the Federal Gardner-Pingree House (1804), and the Derby-Beebe Summer House (c. 1799). The museum's new wing includes an interactive center for children and families. A shop and café are also on the premises (1-800-745-4054, www.pem.org).

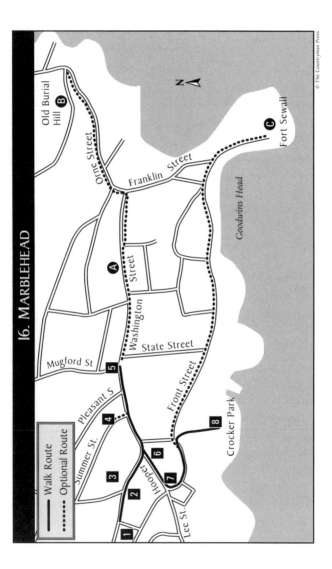

16. MARBLEHEAD

16 · Marblehead

Directions: *By car:* Take MA 128 north to exit 25A (MA 114). Then take MA 114 east. *By public transportaion:* From the MBTA Haymarket T station take MBTA bus 441/442. Or, from the MBTA Downtown Crossing T station take MBTA bus 442/449 (1-800-392-6100, www.mbta.com).

Fishermen from Cornwall, England, and the English Channel Islands came to this rocky peninsula in 1629. In colonial times Marblehead was a major port and a shipbuilding center.

Begin this walking tour of Marblehead by viewing its most famous artwork—*The Spirit of '76*. Painted by Archibald M. Willard, it was put on display at the Centennial Celebration in Philadelphia in 1876. It is now permanently exhibited at Abbot Hall (1), Marblehead's Victorian, red brick town hall, built in 1876 and located in Washington Square. The artist's models were his father (the drummer), an old soldier (the fifer), and a local schoolboy (the second drummer). The painting has become one of America's best-known works of art and a symbol of our national heritage. In addition to the painting there are a number of historic items to see at Abbot Hall (781-631-0000, www.marblehead.com).

Exit Abbot Hall on Washington Street. Turn right

and walk down the street to the Historical Society's J.O.J. Frost Folk Art Gallery (2) at number 170. Frost painted scenes of Marblehead, many of which are exhibited at the gallery (781-631-1768, www.essexheritage.org/jeremiah_lee.htm).

Cross the street to the 1768 Jeremiah Lee Mansion (3) at 161 Washington Street. The house was built for the wealthy merchant and patriot Colonel Jeremiah Lee and is considered one of the premier examples of Georgian architecture on this side of the Atlantic. The rusticated facade features wood cut to resemble stone blocks. Sand was mixed into the exterior paint so that the blocks not only look, but feel like stone as well. The mansion's interior has original, hand-printed English wallpaper and period furnishings. There is a permanent exhibit of Marblehead pottery, paintings, nautical memorabilia, military objects, and folk art. The gardens have been restored to their 18th-century splendor. The entire site is opened to the public by the Marblehead Historical Society (781-631-1768, www.essexheritage.org/jeremiah_lee.htm).

After seeing the Lee Mansion turn left and continue down Washington Street. St. Michael's Episcopal Church (4) will be on the left at 13 Summer Street. Built in 1714 and enlarged in 1728, this is the oldest Episcopal church building in New England and the second oldest in America. On the interior note the reredos, the altar screen, which dates to colonial times. The English brass chandelier was hung in 1732. The tower bell was cast at Paul Revere's foundry (781-631-0657).

From St. Michael's continue down Washington Street to the old Town House (5) at Market Square, another Georgian building, this one built in 1727. Note the quoins (false-stone corner blocks). Pre-Revolutionary town meetings were held here, and so this has become known as Marblehead's "Cradle of Liberty."

Option A: Old North Church is farther down Washington Street just beyond Pearl Street. Its congregation gathered in 1635, and the present church was built in 1824. Atop the steeple note the gilded codfish weathervane, which predates the church itself.

Option B: The Old Burial Ground is a bit farther on. At the end of Washington Street bear left onto Orne Street. The cemetery will be on the left. Old Burial Hill was first used in 1638 and was the site of the first two meetinghouses of the Old North Church congregation. The Burial Ground contains hundreds of 17th- and 18th-century graves, including those of six hundred Revolutionary War soldiers. Fountain Park is across the street. There are breathtaking views of the harbor from both the Burial Ground and the park.

Cross Washington Street and reverse your direction. The Robert King Hooper Mansion (6) will be on your left at 8 Hooper Street. The mansion was built for "merchant prince" Robert Hooper in 1728. He was nicknamed "King Hooper," perhaps because his vast wealth allowed him to live like royalty. The Georgian front rooms and rusticated facade date from 1745. The most interesting features of the interior, however, are the ballroom and the wine cellar. The Marblehead Arts Association mounts changing exhibits in the mansion (781-631-2608, www.marbleheadarts.org).

After seeing the Hooper Mansion turn left and walk to the corner of Hooper and Union Streets. There you will see a curiosity known as the Lafayette House (7). Note that the corner has been cut from the house. Local folklore has it that this part of the house was cut and removed in 1824 to allow easy passage for General Lafayette's large carriage as he went by while touring Marblehead.

Union Street will lead you to Front Street. Bear left onto Front and Crocker Park (8) will be on your right. Visit the park and enjoy the panoramic views of Marblehead Harbor.

Option C: Fort Sewall is at the end of Front Street. Built in 1742, the fort remained active through the Spanish American War. It is now a park affording visitors unrivaled views of the harbor, the ocean, and the lighthouse on Marblehead Neck.

17 · Rockport

Directions: *By car:* Take MA 128 north to the end of the route in Gloucester. Then take MA 127 north to Rockport. *By public transportation:* Take the MBTA Commuter Rail from North Station (1-800-392-6100, www.mbta.com).

Rockport is located on Cape Ann, which is named for the wife of the British King James I. The tour begins in Dock Square (1). As you face the bay Bearskin Neck (2) will be on your right. According to the historic marker, Bearskin Neck was ". . . named for a bear caught by the tide and killed in 1700. Commercial and ship building center of Rockport for 150 years. First dock built here in 1743." Bearskin Neck is now a tourist mecca, covered with many shops and eateries. Should you walk the length of the neck you will be rewarded with views of Sandy Bay and Rockport Harbor at Old Stone Fort. The fort built during the War of 1812 no longer stands but the site still bears its name. As you walk the Neck Motif #1 (3) will be on your right on Bradley Wharf. The motif, a fisherman's shack hung with colorful buoys, is a favorite subject for artists and is said to be the most painted and photographed building in America. The present Motif #1 is a replica that replaces an earlier building washed away during the Blizzard of 1978.

17. ROCKPORT

Return to Dock Square. Continue through the square and onto Main Street. Stop at 12 Main Street, on the left. This is the Old Tavern, built in the 1780s. The Rockport Art Association now uses the Tavern as gallery space for changing exhibits by local artists (978-546-6604).

The First Congregational Church, also known as Old Sloop (4), is just beyond School Street on the left. The congregation first gathered in 1755, and the present church was built in 1804. The next church building (just beyond Cleaves Street) is the Unitarian Universalist Church. The Universalist Benevolent Society in Rockport was founded in 1821; the present church was built eight years later.

Leave Main Street when you reach Beach Street, turning to the left. Front and Back Beaches (farther on) both offer superb views of Sandy Bay. Visit the Old Burial Ground (5) on your left and the adjacent Millbrook Meadow. Walk down King Street to the Sandy Bay Historical Society and Museums (6), housed in the Sewell-Scripture House (1832) at 40 King Street. Allow time to see the exhibits: period rooms, ship models and maritime memorabilia, paintings, costumes, glass, and other objects of historic interest. The society also opens the Old Castle—a 1715 saltbox close by at the corner of Granite and Curtis Streets (978-546-9533, www.sbhs-rockport.org).

18 · Newburyport

Directions: *By car:* Take I-95 north to exit 57. Follow the signs to downtown Newburyport. *By public transportation:* Take MBTA Commuter Rail from North Station (1-800-392-6100, www.mbta.com). Three bus lines have service between Boston and Newburyport: C&J Trailways (1-800-258-7111, www.cjtrailways.com); The Coach Co. (1-800-874-3377, www.coachco.com); Vermont Transit (1-800-642-3133, www.vermonttransit.com).

The English settled Newbury in 1635 and in 1764 the port became a separate town. Ideally situated at the mouth of the Merrimack River, Newburyport thrived in colonial times and became a major shipbuilding center. Following the Revolution shipbuilding continued, reaching its height in the 1840s, when clipper ships were built in the town's shipyards.

The walking tour starts at Waterfront Park (1) with a fine view of the Merrimack River. Walk just a few steps to the Firehouse Center for the Performing and Visual Arts (2). The center is in an 1823 red brick structure that was built as a lyceum. It has also been used as a market house and fire station. Restored in 1980, the Firehouse Center is Newburyport's nucleus for the arts and con-

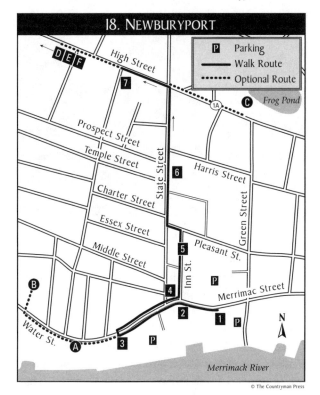

18. NEWBURYPORT

P	Parking
——	Walk Route
••••••	Optional Route

High Street

Prospect Street

Temple Street

Charter Street

Essex Street

Middle Street

State Street

Harris Street

Green Street

Pleasant St.

Inn St.

Merrimac Street

Water St.

Frog Pond

Merrimack River

N

© The Countryman Press

tains a theater, art gallery, and restaurant (978-462-7336, www.firehousecenter.com).

The Firehouse Center faces Water Street. With your back to the center turn left and walk down Water Street. On your left will be the Atkinson Building. A mid-nineteenth-century Italianate design, its facade is red brick and cast iron. Stop at the Old Custom House Maritime Museum (3) on your left, a monumental 1835 granite building. Its architect, Robert Mills, designed similar custom houses for New Bedford, Massachusetts (see

Inn Street

page 109), and New London, Connecticut. His best-known work is the Washington Memorial in Washington, D.C. Step inside the museum. Its collection focuses on Newburyport's history and maritime paintings, artwork, and memorabilia (978-462-8681).

Option A: The Newburyport Art Association is just a few doors down at 65 Water Street. It is situated in a two-hundred-year-old waterfront warehouse, which has been renovated to gallery space for works by local artists (978-465-8769, www.newburyportart.org).

Option B: The Tannery is on Water Street between Independent and Federal Streets. This cluster of old mill buildings, revitalized and renovated, now houses an art gallery, shops, and restaurants.

Reverse direction and walk up Water Street to Market Square (4). It was here that colonists burned tea in 1773 to protest British taxation. Inn Street, one of the oldest byways in this port city, starts at Market Square. Now a pedestrian mall, it is an award-winning urban renewal project. Walk the length of the street from Market Square to Pleasant Street. Turn left onto Pleasant Street and walk to State Street. During the Civil War army headquarters was at 57 State Street. Turn right and walk up State Street. The Newburyport Public Library (6) is at number 94; its original wing dates to 1771. Opposite the library, the Dalton House (at number 95), built in 1792, was home to Massachusetts' first U.S. Senator, Tristam Dalton.

Option C: When you reach the corner of State and High Streets make a right. Bartlett Mall, a park, will be on your left. The Superior Court Building (1805) is attributed to Charles Bulfinch. On the far side of the Frog Pond are the Old County Jail (1823) and the Old Hill Burying Ground.

Return to High Street and walk to the corner of Fruit Street. The Cushing House Museum and Garden (7) will be on your left at 98 High Street. Built in 1808, this twenty-room house was home to the Cushing family until 1955, when it was given to the Historical Society of Old Newbury. The red brick house, forty feet on each side, is an excellent example of a Federal-style house. Its interior has the atmosphere of an affluent New England shipowner's home and is a treasure trove of period furnishings, portraits, maritime memorabilia, a clock collection, and objects collected on overseas voyages. The house is a National Historic Landmark. Its garden has been restored to its late-19th-century design (978-462-2681).

The three options below extend this walking tour. Each of the properties is owned and maintained by the Society for the Preservation of New England Antiquities (978-462-2634, www.spnea.org).

Option D: The Coffin House (c. 1654) is about a mile farther down High Street, which becomes High Road (MA 1A). After seeing the Cushing House and Garden, face High Street, turn left, and walk down the street. The Coffin House will be on your left at 14 High Road, Newbury. The house is a compendium of 17th-, 18th-, and 19-century New England architecture. What began as a diminutive post-medieval timber two-room dwelling later grew and was divided to accommodate successive generations of the Coffin family.

Option E: The Swett-Ilsley house is steps away at 4 High Road. Built in the mid-1600s, the house did not stay in the same family, but rather had a series of owners, each modifying the structure according to their needs. The Swett-Ilsley house is a SPNEA study house and may be toured by appointment only.

Option F: Less than one mile farther along High Road is the Spencer-Pierce-Little Farm (c. 1690). At Little's Lane turn left to the farm entrance. Unlike the Coffin and Swett-Ilsley Houses, which were initially modest timber farmhouses, this was built as a stone-and-brick manorhouse. Throughout the 18th and early 19th centuries it was the country estate of wealthy merchants. In the mid-1800s the Little family established a farm on the estate. The house is filled with period furnishings, and excavated artifacts are on exhibit. After visiting the house you may want to explore the property on the Eliza Little Walking Trail.

19 · Lowell

Directions: *By car:* From MA 128 take MA 3 north to the Lowell Connector. Take exit 5B, Thorndike Street. Follow Thorndike Street through four traffic lights. *By public transportation:* Take MBTA Commuter Rail from North Station to Lowell (1-800-362-6100, www.mbta.com). It is a short cab ride from the station to the beginning of this tour. Alternately, there is bus service from South Station through Vermont Transit (1-800-642-3133, www.vermonttransit.com) or Peter Pan Bus Lines (1-800-343-9999, www.peterpanbus.com). Once in Lowell at the Gallagher Transportation Terminal, it is a very short cab ride to the American Textile Museum and the beginning of this tour.

English settlers came to this area in 1653 and named it East Chelmsford. It remained an area of farms along the Concord and Merrimack Rivers until the Industrial Revolution. The mighty water power of Pawtucket Falls was harnessed, textile mills were built, and a canal system set in place that connected the mills to each other and to Boston. In 1826 Lowell was incorporated, named for textile magnate Francis Cabot Lowell, and became known as the Spindle City. Charles Dickens visited Lowell and wrote about "the Manchester of America."

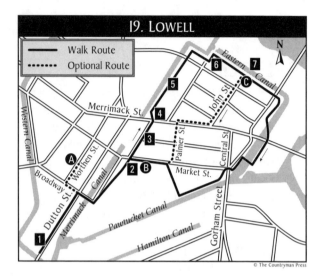

19. LOWELL

— Walk Route
••••••• Optional Route

N

Western Canal
Merrimack St.
Worthen St.
Dutton St.
Broadway
Merrimack Canal
Pawtucket Canal
Hamilton Canal
Palmer St.
Market St.
John St.
Central St.
Gorham Street
Eastern Canal

A B C 1 2 3 4 5 6 7

© The Countryman Press

The tour begins at the American Textile History Museum (1) at 491 Dutton Street. The museum began in 1960 in North Andover, Massachusetts, and moved to this historic mill building in 1997. It is the world's largest textile museum, with almost one hundred exhibits that illustrate the textile industry in America in the 18th and 19th centuries. Clothing, fabrics, hand-powered tools, and machinery are on display. Exhibits include an 18th-century weaver's log cabin and an operating woolen mill from the 1870s. Special exhibits are mounted throughout the year. A café and shop are on the premises (978-441-0400, www.athm.org).

Option A: To visit the Whistler House Museum of Art, walk down Dutton Street, parallel to the trolley track. Turn left onto Broadway Street and then right onto Worthen Street. The Whistler House will be on the left. American artist James McNeill Whistler was born in this house on July 11, 1834. His father, Major George Washington Whistler, was a civil engineer working on Lowell's canals. His mother, of course, is the subject of the artist's best-known work, *Arrangement in Grey and Black, No.1: The Artist's Mother,* more commonly known as Whistler's Mother. The house, built in 1823, was opened as a museum in 1908 by the Lowell Art Association. One permanent exhibit tells the story of the artist's life. Another displays a number of his prints. Other permanent exhibits focus on 19th-century New England art and works by Lowell artists past and present (978-452-7641, www.whistlerhouse.org).

An interesting aside: The neighborhood just in back of the Whistler House is known as the Acre—Lowell's ethnic neighborhood. The Acre was originally settled by Irish immigrants, who were later joined by Greeks. From Whistler House you may see the Acre's two large church landmarks: the granite, Gothic Revival St. Patrick's Church (1831) and the massive gilded dome of Holy Trinity Greek Orthodox Church (1907). Reflecting more recent waves of immigration, the Acre is also populated by Hispanics and Southeast Asians today.

Cross the Merrimack Canal on Market Street to the Lowell National Historic Park Visitor Center (2), located in Market Mills. The park includes museums and restored, 19th-century mills, gatehouses, and over five miles of canals. While this is a walking tour, the park service does offer alternatives: trolleys and canal boats. If you wish to explore these options, speak with one of the park rangers (978-970-5000, www.nps.gov/lowe).

Option B: The Brush Art Gallery and Studios is adjacent to the visitors center. You may visit the galleries and watch artists at work in their studios, or shop. (978-

459-7819, www.go.boston.com/brushartgallery).

When you leave Market Mills cross Market Street and walk down Shattuck Street. The New England Quilt Museum (3) will be on the right at number 18. Built in 1845, for many years this building housed the Lowell Institution for Savings. A museum since 1993, it houses changing exhibits of antique, traditional, and contemporary quilts, as well as a reference library and museum shop (978-452-4207, www.nequiltmuseum.org).

Shattuck Street ends at Merrimack Street—one of Lowell's main thoroughfares which today is dotted with dozens of restaurants and upscale shops.

Opposite the intersection of Merrimack and Shattuck Streets is St. Anne's Episcopal Church (4), founded in 1825. James McNeill Whistler was baptized here. The bell tower houses a chime of eleven bells that dates to 1857. Inside, the stained-glass windows (some by Tiffany and others by Connick) light the Gothic Revival nave. The Hook and Hastings organ was installed in 1884 (978-452-2150, www.ultranet.com/~stannes).

Two city halls are visible from the step of St. Anne's. Directly across the street (at Merrimack and Shattuck Streets) is the old, red brick, early-19th-century city hall. To the right and is the granite tower of the present, century-old city hall.

Continue north along the Merrimack Canal (5). As you progress along this, the Canalway Trail of the National Park Service, you will see it is punctuated by a series of wayside exhibits that recount Lowell's history.

Stop at the Boot Mills Boarding House and Morgan Cultural Center (6). The Working People Exhibit concentrates on the lives of mill girls, immigrants, and others who labored here. The Boarding House also con-

Boot Cotton Mills Museum

tains the Center for Lowell History (978-970-5000, www.nps.gov/lowe).

Boarding House Park is an outdoor amphitheater used for concerts, theatrical presentations, and special events.

Cross Eastern Canal and visit the Boot Cotton Mills Museum (7). The museum has a large and impressive weave room filled with dozens of operating, 1920s power looms. Ear plugs are provided by the park service! There are also interactive exhibits and videos, all retelling Lowell's history.

Option C: At the Boot Mills trolley stop you may board a trolley bound for the Suffolk Mill Turbine Exhibit, which demonstrates how power was generated from a thirteen-foot fall of water in the canal (978-970-5000, www.nps.gov/lowe).

From the Boot Cotton Mills Museum continue to follow the Canalway Trail back to the visitors center, stopping at wayside exhibits along the way.

20 · Andover

Directions: *By car:* Take I-93 north to exit 41. At the end of the ramp turn right and take MA 125 east for two miles. Then turn right (north) onto MA 28, North Main Street. *By public transportation:* Take the MBTA Commuter Rail to Andover (1-800-392-6100, www.mbta.com) or Trombley Bus Lines (1-800-640-8766, www.trombleybuslines.com).

To the Indians this area was known as *Cochichewick*, the Great Cascade. Colonists from Andover, England, came here in 1642 and renamed the site. Though textile mills flourished in 19th-century Andover, the town is best known for Phillips Academy, one of the oldest preparatory schools in the nation. It was founded for boys in 1778; a sister school, Abbot Female Academy, was opened in 1829. The schools merged in 1973. A third school here is Andover Theological Seminary.

Begin your walk through Andover at the 1819 Amos Blanchard House Museum (1) at 97 Main Street, a very good example of the houses built for the growing New England middle-class early in the 19th century. The interior of this Federal house has been restored to its appearance during the period from 1820 to 1840. Also visit the Barn Museum. The English-style barn contains a permanent exhibit of 19th-century tools as well as

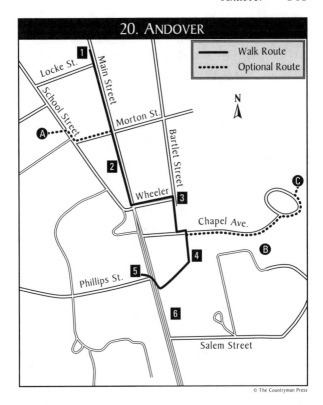

20. ANDOVER

Locke St.

Main Street

School Street

Morton St.

Bartlet Street

Wheeler

Chapel Ave.

Phillips St.

Salem Street

— Walk Route

········ Optional Route

N

1 2 3 4 5 6

A B C

© The Countryman Press

changing exhibits. The Andover Historical Society maintains the house, barn museum, a library, and a research center (978-475-2236, www.ultranet.com/~andhists).

Walk south on Main Street toward the Andover Hill National Register Historic District.

Option A: To visit the campus built for Abbot Academy, turn right onto Morton Street and then right again onto School Street. Abbot Circle will be on the left. The Circle was designed and landscaped by Frederick Law

Olmsted whose most famous works are Manhattan's Central Park, Boston's Emerald Necklace, and Brooklyn's Prospect Park. Surrounding the Circle are Abbot Hall (1829), Draper Hall (1890), and McKeenan Hall (1904).

Walk back to Main Street. Turn right (south) onto Main Street and stop at number 147. This is known as America House (2), because the song "America" ("My country 'tis of thee") was composed here in 1832 by Samuel F. Smith. Smith boarded in this house while a student at Andover Theological Seminary. The melody has its roots in England ("God Save the Queen"), but the lyrics Smith wrote have become one of this nation's favorite patriotic songs. A dormitory, America House is not open to visitors.

Continue to walk down Main Street and turn left at the next corner onto Bartlet Street. Harriet Beecher Stowe lived in the stone house at 80 Bartlet Street (3). Stowe's husband was a minister and a faculty member at Andover Theological Seminary, and they lived here for a time in the 1850s. It was also at this time that her most famous work, *Uncle Tom's Cabin*, became popular and advanced the abolitionists' cause. Now faculty housing, the house is not open to the public. Facing 80 Bartlett Street make a right and walk to Chapel Avenue.

Option B: To visit Stowe's grave, turn left onto Chapel Avenue. The Chapel Cemetery will be on the right. From the entry gate walk straight down the path to the middle of the cemetery.

Option C: The Moncrieff Corcoran Sanctuary is nearby. The 80-acre parcel is a quiet, wooded area intersected with walking paths, flowering trees and shrubs, two tranquil ponds, and birds and other wildlife. To reach the sanctuary walk to the end of Chapel Avenue to the circle. The entry is marked by two stone gateposts.

The green between the chapel and the Memorial Bell Tower (1923) was created in the 1920s and 1930s. As you look across the campus the Addison Gallery of American Art (4) is on the left. The gallery has twelve thousand objects in its collection, from paintings, sculpture, and prints, to photographs and decorative arts. The list of American artists represented in the gallery is impressive, including John Singleton Copley, Thomas Eakins, Winslow Homer, and James McNeill Whistler. Twentieth-century artists include Edward Hopper, Alexander Calder, Georgia O'Keefe, Jackson Pollack, Andrew Wyeth, and Phillips alumnus Frank Stella. In addition to its permanent collection the gallery mounts about nine special exhibits each year (978-749-4015, www.andover.edu).

The path from the gallery leads diagonally to the left. Cross the street to the Robert S. Peabody Museum of Archaeology (5). A plaque on the outside identifies this as the site of the first Phillips Academy building. Founded in 1901 and named for benefactor Robert S. Peabody (Phillips class of 1857), the museum has a collection of more than seven hundred thousand artifacts from nearly every North American indigenous people. The world's largest collection of Native American baskets is in the collection, as well as weapons, clothing and textiles, pottery, and utensils. Archaeologic and photographic collections complete the museum's holdings (978-749-4490, www.andover.edu).

After visiting the museum look your right across the street. The sculpture is known as the *Armillary Sphere* (6). A sundial, it is the work of Paul Manship and was created in 1928. It stands in front of the Oliver Wendell Holmes Library. Holmes was a Phillips Academy alumnus (class of 1825). The library has over one hundred thousand books—the largest holding of any secondary school in the country.

21 · Worcester

Directions: *By car:* Take I-90, the Massachusetts Turnpike, west to exit 8, then I-290 east to exit 16. After exiting turn left onto Central Street and then left onto Main Street. City Hall and the common will be on the left after two traffic lights. *By public transportation:* Two bus companies offer service from Boston: Peter Pan Bus Lines (1-800-343-9999, www. peterpanbus.com) and Greyhound Lines (1-800-231-2222, www.greyhound.com).

Worcester is named for Worcester, England. Begin at the Common (1) planned in 1669 by the first settlers for use as public pasture, burial ground, and as a site for the meetinghouse and school. Today the Common is flanked by the Worcester Common Outlets Mall on one side and City Hall on the other. Built in 1898, City Hall replaces an earlier hall that stood on this site. The firm of Peabody and Stearns designed the Italian Renaissance Revival building. Note the Florentine tower that rises over two hundred feet. A plaque on the sidewalk marks the spot where the Declaration of Independence was first read in New England on July 14, 1776.

From the door of City Hall turn right and walk down Main Street. Then turn left onto Elm Street. The Worcester Historical Museum and Library (2) is at 30 Elm

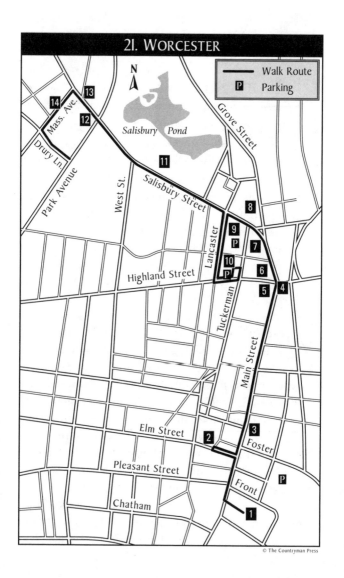

21. WORCESTER

Walk Route
P Parking

N

Salisbury Pond

Grove Street

Park Avenue

Mass. Ave.

Drury Ln.

West St.

Salisbury Street

Lancaster

Highland Street

Tuckerman

Main Street

Elm Street

Foster

Pleasant Street

Front

Chatham

13 **14** **12** **11** **8** **9** **P** **7** **10** **P** **6** **5** **4** **2** **3** **1**

© The Countryman Press

Street. Founded in 1875, the museum documents the city's history; hundreds of objects are on display. A permanent exhibit, In Their Shirtsleeves, focuses on the Industrial Revolution and Worcester's industrialists, inventors, and working people. Changing exhibits are mounted featuring many aspects of the city's history, from the earliest settlement to the present (508-753-8278, www.worcesterhistory.org).

Return to Main Street. Turn left and stop at Mechanics Hall (3), at number 321. An outstanding example of Italianate design, this auditorium was built in 1857 and is recognized as the best concert hall built in America before the Civil War. Restored in 1975, Mechanics Hall is a National Historic Landmark. Its auditorium has excellent acoustics, and there are concerts and performances by world-class artists (508-752-5608, www.mechanicshall.com).

Walk to the opposite end of Main Street and Lincoln Square. (You may wish to drive to Lincoln Square, since there is little of note between it and Mechanics Hall. Main Street, by and large, is a shadow of its former self.)

Lincoln Square (4) was a site of commercial activity in colonial times; a tavern, a mill, a jailhouse, and stores (one of which is on this tour) were clustered here. The Worcester County Courthouse (5) sits at the corner of Main and Highland Streets. This is the fourth courthouse on this site. Note the 1853 Greek Revival wing on the left. The later additions, all classical revival, were added in 1898. Nearby, the limestone Municipal War Memorial Auditorium (6) was built in 1933 as a World War I memorial.

Beyond Lincoln Square Salisbury Street curves to the left. Tuckerman Hall (7), originally known as the

Worcester Women's Club, is on the left. Worcester was the site of the first national women's rights convention in 1850. In 1880, following an observance of the convention's anniversary, the Worcester Women's Club was founded. The architect chosen for the building was Josephine Wright Chapman—one of America's first female architects. The clubhouse was built in 1902. In 1981 it was acquired by the Central Massachusetts Symphony Orchestra and restored in 1999. Tuckerman Hall is unique: a triangular building on a triangular lot, with round towers at each corner. The interior has an elegant 550-seat theater, a circular 200-seat auditorium, and tower suites reflecting a wide variety of decorative styles: American Colonial, Italian Renaissance, Dutch, and Moorish. Under the auspices of the Central Massachusetts Symphony Orchestra, concerts and special events take place year-round (508-754-1234).

Continue up Salisbury Street; the Worcester Armory (8) will be on the right at number 44. The armory houses three museums: the Massachusetts National Guard Military Archives and Museum, the American Division Museum, and the Worcester Fire Department Museum (508-797-0334).

The Worcester Art Museum (9) is at 55 Salisbury Street, between Tuckerman and Lancaster Streets. It was founded in 1896 by Stephen Salisbury III, who donated the land and bequeathed a generous endowment. Enter the museum through the 1933 Aldrich addition, which leads to the original 1897 galleries. The museum was further expanded in 1970 and again in 1983. Both the building and the collection are impressive. On entering the museum you are greeted by a large, central, Renaissance courtyard that is surrounded by galleries.

The art on display spans five thousand years, and much of it is presented in chronological order: Egyptian through Classical, medieval, and up to the present. A highlight of the collection is a vaulted 12th-century Romanesque chapter house that was transported, stone by stone, from a French monastery. The medieval collection also includes paintings, stained-glass windows, frescoes, sculpture, and ivories. There are European works from the Renaissance, 17th-century Dutch and Flemish artists (including Rembrandt and Rubens), late-19th- and 20th-century European artists (including Picasso, Matisse, Cezanne),and contemporary artists. The American art collection spans the 17th to the 21st centuries. A well-known, outstanding American painting in the collection is the 17th-century *Portrait of Mrs. Freake and Baby Mary*, whose artist is unkown. Pre-Columbian, Persian, Islamic, and Asian art complete the holdings. Special exhibits are mounted periodically (508-799-4406, www.worcesterart.org).

From the museum walk down Lancaster Street and turn left onto Highland Street. The Salisbury Mansion (10) will be on the left. Built on Lincoln Square in 1772 and used as a store, it was converted for use as an elegant house for the Salisburys in 1819. It was moved from Lincoln Square to Highland Street in 1929 and today is opened to the public by the Worcester Historical Museum (508-753-8278, www.worcesterhistory.org).

As you face the front door of the Salisbury Mansion look to the right. The smaller building, also a Salisbury-owned store in Lincoln Square, was moved here in 1929. Farther to the right is a Greek Revival house built in 1836 for Stephen Salisbury II. Neither of these buildings are open to the public.

Return to the Worcester Art Museum and resume your walk up Salisbury Street. Institute Park (11) will be on the right. The 17-acre parcel was the gift of Stephen Salisbury III.

Opposite the park, on the left, is the Worcester Polytechnic Institute. Founded in 1868, it was one of the first schools of science and engineering in America.

Just beyond Park Avenue, on the left, is the American Antiquarian Society (12), founded in 1821. The Georgian Revival building, designed by Winslow, Bigelow, and Wadsworth in 1909, is a national research library of American culture and history from colonial times until 1876 (508-755-5221, www.americanantiquarian.org).

A stone marker (13) at the corner of Salisbury Street and Montvale Road commemorates the birthplace of George Bancroft, founder of the U.S. Naval Academy in Annapolis, Maryland.

Massachusetts Avenue (14) begins at Salisbury Street; it was developed in 1899. Walk down the avenue and stop at number 6. This Georgian structure was built in 1751 in Lincoln Square, then was moved to this site and converted to use as a house in 1899. Continue your walk down Massachusetts Avenue, turn left onto Drury Lane, and conclude your tour.

22 · Springfield

Directions: *By car:* Take I-90, the Massachusetts Turnpike, west to exit 6, and I-291 south. Take exit 2A (Main Street). Turn left onto Main Street and then right onto Court Street. The campanile will be on your right. *By public transportation:* Peter Pan Bus Lines (1-800-343-9999, www.peterpanbus.com), Vermont Transit (1-800-642-3133, www.vermonttransit.com), and Bonanza Bus Lines (1-888-751-8800, www.bonanzabus.com) all offer service to Springfield.

Englishman William Pynchon founded Springfield in 1636 and named it for his birthplace in Britain. The opening of the Arsenal in 1777 launched Springfield into the Industrial Revolution, transforming it from a farming to a manufacturing center. The Arsenal grew and increased its production significantly during the Civil War. A National Historic Site, the Arsenal is a destination on this tour.

The tour begins at the city's most visible landmark: the 300-foot-tall campanile at City Hall (1). Built in 1913 and designed by Pelland Corbett, it houses a peel of twelve bells. Flanking the tower are two granite classical revival buildings with twin Corinthian porticoes: City Hall and Symphony Hall.

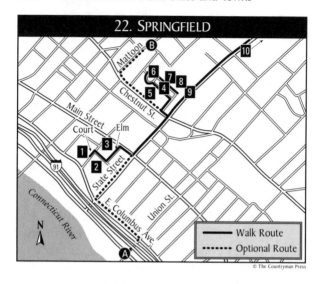

Cross Court Street to the Old First Church (2). The first meetinghouse was built on this site in 1645. It was replaced by a series of increasingly larger churches in 1677, 1752, and then finally with the present one in 1819. Note the rooster weathervane on top of the cupola. Four feet high and weighing 60 pounds, it was made in London in 1750. The Old First Church is on the National Historic Register.

The church faces Court Square (3), which in earlier times was known as Meeting House Square. At the foot of Court Square turn right onto Main Street and walk to State Street.

Option A: The Basketball Hall of Fame is in the neighborhood at 1150 West Columbus Avenue. The game was invented in Springfield in 1891 by James Naismith, a YMCA instructor. The hall of fame's museum documents the game's history from its the very beginning to the present with memorabilia, displays, and interactive exhibits (413-781-6500, www.hoophall.com).

Walk to the corner of State and Chestnut Streets. Cross to *The Puritan*, a well-known statue modeled in the 1880s by American artist Augustus Saint-Gaudens. It depicts Deacon Samuel Chapin (1595–1675), one of Springfield's founding fathers, marching forward with a bible in one hand and a walking stick in the other, and wearing a pilgrim's broad-rimmed hat and ample cape. The statue was restored in 1995 through the generosity of one of Chapin's descendants.

Venture into the Quadrangle behind the *Puritan*. There you'll see a delightful group of five statues, all combined to form the Dr. Seuss Memorial Sculpture Garden (4). One of Springfield's favorite sons, Dr. Seuss, born Theodor Seuss Geisel in 1904, became the author of many beloved children's books including *The Cat in the Hat, Green Eggs and Ham,* and *How the Grinch Stole Christmas.* Seuss died in 1991. His stepdaughter, Lark Grey Dimond-Cates, modeled the five bronze sculptures, which represent the author and some of his best-known characters, among them the Cat in the Hat, Horton the Elephant, and Yertle the Turtle. The memorial was unveiled in May 2002.

The Quadrangle has an outstanding group of public buildings of various styles and purposes. Starting clockwise, on the left is Christ Church Cathedral. An Episcopal parish since its founding in 1817, the brownstone Norman-style church (1876) was elevated to cathedral status in 1929. The wooden pulpit and lectern were carved by the renowned Kirshmayer and its stained-glass windows designed by John Lafarge (413-736-2742, www.christchurchcathedralspringfield.org).

SPRINGFIELD LIBRARY & MUSEUMS ASSOCIATION

Dr. Seuss Sculpture Garden

Walk to the Museum of Fine Arts (5). Founded in 1933, its central interior work is the facade of a 16th-century Spanish palace. There are galleries devoted to American, Italian, French, English, Dutch, and Flemish art. (All of the museums in the Quadrangle share the same contact information: 413-263-6800, 1-800-625-7738, www.quadrangle.org).

The Connecticut Valley Historical Museum (6) is at the northern end of the Quadrangle. Featuring the social history of the region, the museum also includes the Genealogy and Local History Library.

Continuing clockwise around the Quadrangle the Springfield Science Museum (7) will be next on the left. Museum highlights include a planetarium, an eco-center with aquarium and live animals, and exhibits on many subjects, such as dinosaurs, Africa, and early aviation. Many of the exhibits are interactive.

The George Walter Vincent Smith Art Museum (8) is just south of the Science Museum. Built in 1895, the Italian Renaissance–style structure was designed by James Renwick Jr., whose best-known works are the Smithsonian Castle in Washington D.C. and St. Patrick's Cathedral in New York City. Smith was a New Yorker who retired to Springfield and donated his art collection to the city's Library Association in 1889. There is a good collection of American paintings, especially works by Hudson River School artists. There is also a good collection of Asian art, which includes a Shinto shrine and decorative arts.

Your walk around the Quadrangle comes to an end at the Springfield Central Library (9). Another Italian Renaissance design, the Vermont marble building was completed in 1912.

Option B: Mattoon Street, a National Historic District, is just two blocks north of the Quadrangle. It is lined with restored Victorian row houses, most of which were built between 1870 and 1890. Grace Baptist Church, designed by Henry Hobson Richardson, stands at the head of the street.

After visiting the Quadrangle return to State Street,

turn left, and climb up the hill. Roman Catholic St. Michael's Cathedral will be on the left. Within two blocks the Springfield Armory National Historic Site (10) will be on the left. Enter the armory by making a left on Federal Street.

The site for the armory was chosen by George Washington in 1777. At first it was a storage facility for munitions. In 1787 an episode in Shays Rebellion took place here: Daniel Shays and his men tried to seize the arms. Muskets were manufactured here starting in 1795, and during the Civil War the arsenal produced about one thousand rifles a day. Longfellow visited and then wrote "The Arsenal at Springfield," poetically referring to the Organ of Rifles, which resembled organ pipes.

The Arsenal is opened to the public by the National Park Service. Covering 55 acres, it includes the Main Arsenal (1847), where the world's largest collection of small arms is on display; an earlier arsenal; and two houses, the Commanding Officer's Quarters (1846) and the Master Armorer's House, built in 1833 (413-734-8551, www.nps.gov/spar).

23 · Amherst

Directions: *By car:* Take I-90, the Massachusetts Turnpike, west to exit 4, then I-91 north to exit 19, then MA 9 east to Amherst. *By public transportation:* Use Peter Pan Bus Lines (1-800-343-9999, www.peterpanbus.com) or AMTRAK (1800-USA-RAIL, www.amtrak.com). Alternate transportation from Springfield is provided through Valley Transporter (1-800-872-8752 or 413-253-1350).

The area was first settled by the British in the 1730s. Amherst was incorporated in 1776 and took its name from Baron Jeffrey Amherst, a British commander during the French and Indian War. Noah Webster, Emily Dickinson, and Robert Frost all made Amherst their home. Amherst College was founded in 1821 and the University of Massachusetts was founded here in 1863.

The tour starts at the Amherst History Museum (1), in the Strong House at 67 Amity Street. Built in 1774, this is one of the oldest houses in the valley. A larger wing was added in the late 18th century, and the building has many Georgian, Federal, and Victorian details. The museum includes period rooms and exhibits of arts and artifacts representing nearly three hundred years of local history (413-256-0678, www.amhersthistory.org).

Next door is the Jones Library (2) at 43 Amity Street.

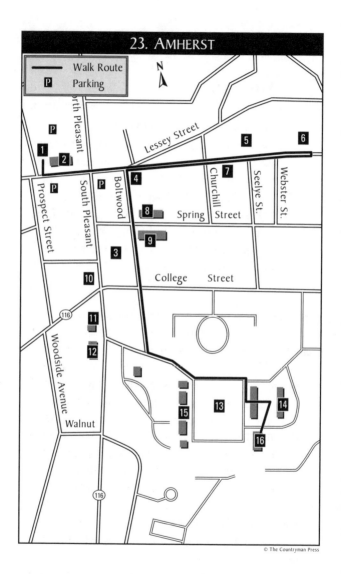

23. AMHERST

Walk Route
P Parking

N

North Pleasant

Lessey Street

Prospect Street

South Pleasant

Boltwood

Churchill Street

Seelye St.

Webster St.

Spring Street

College Street

Woodside Avenue

Walnut

116

116

© The Countryman Press

Designed and built in 1928 to resemble a large private home, the gambrel-roofed structure has a facade of field stones gathered and set into place by Italian stonecutters. The Special Collections Department has eight thousand items on Emily Dickinson, eleven thousand on Robert Frost, and other collections related to local history and genealogy. The library is on the National Register of Historic Places (413-256-4090, www.joneslibrary.org).

From the library continue along Amity Street and cross South Pleasant Street to the beginning of Main Street. The town common (3) is on the right. Set aside for public use in the 1750s, the park was landscaped by Frederick Law Olmsted in 1874.

Before you, at the corner of Main Street and Boltwood Avenue, is Town Hall (4). Built in 1890, the architect was H. S. McKay of Boston, and its style may be labeled as Richardsonian Romanesque.

Continue along Main Street. The Evergreens (5) will be on the left at number 214. This was the home of Emily Dickinson's brother William Austin Dickinson and his wife. Built in 1856, the house is open to visitors (413-542-8161, www.dickinsonhomestead.org/evergreens).

The Dickinson Homestead (6), at 280 Main Street, is the next stop. It was built by Dickinson's grandfather in 1813; she was born here in 1830, lived most of her life here, and died here in 1886. The Homestead, a National Historic Landmark, is open for tours (413-542-8161, www.dickinsonhomestead.org).

After seeing the Homestead retrace your steps to Town Hall. The First Congregational Church (7), built in 1867, will be on the left. This is where the Dickinson family worshiped. At Town Hall turn left onto Boltwood Avenue. Grace Episcopal Church (8) will be on the left. The English Gothic Revival church was built in 1866; the architect was Englishman Henry Dudley.

The Lord Jeffrey Inn (9) is just beyond Grace Church. The inn was built in 1926 and is owned and operated by Amherst College. With your back to the inn look across the common to a white church building. This is the Old First Baptist Church (10). The Greek Revival structure, built in 1835, remained a church until 1964. It is now known as the Town and Country Building and houses shops.

Walk farther on Boltwood Avenue. It leads to the Amherst College campus. Across the common you will see a series of college buildings. The yellow, churchlike building at right is College Hall (11), built in 1828 to serve the First Congregational Church. Emily Dickinson worshiped here for a time. In 1867 the congregation built a new church (the one on Main Street). The college acquired this building and it was remodeled by McKim, Mead, and White in 1905.

The gray stone, Italianate Morgan Hall (12), built in 1852, is to the left of College Hall. This was once a library, and the Dewey Decimal System was devised here by Melvin Dewey. To the left of Morgan Hall is Amherst College President's House. Built in 1834, it was enlarged in 1891 and again in 1932.

As you walk on Boltwood Avenue straight ahead is a statue of Amherst alumnus Henry Ward Beecher (class of 1834). The Octagon (1848) stands in back of the statue.

At the end of Boltwood Avenue take the path on the left, which will lead you to the Freshman Quadrangle

(13). The library, named for Robert Frost, who taught at Amherst, is on the left. The granite Barrett Hall is straight ahead. At Barrett Hall turn right and follow the sign to the Mead Art Museum (14). The college's art collection began in 1839. Today the museum houses nearly fourteen thousand works, which include American, European, Asian, African, Latin American, and ancient art, as well as silver, furniture, textiles, and photographs. The museum is housed in a rambling, modern, red brick building named for its benefactor, William Rutherford Mead (class of 1867). The firm of McKim, Mead, and White designed the building in 1949. It stands on the site formerly occupied by the Stearns Church. The deteriorating church was demolished but its granite and brownstone steeple (1898) was left standing just to the left of the museum's entrance (413-542-2335, www.amherst.edu/~mead).

From the museum, look straight across the Quad to Johnson Chapel (15). The chapel is a red brick Greek Revival design with white trim and topped by a square tower and the American flag. It is flanked by two of the college's oldest dormitories, North College and South College.

Turn left and enter the Pratt Museum of Natural History (16). The museum houses a unique and comprehensive collection of about eighty thousand objects: fossils, minerals, anthropological artifacts, geologic phenomena, and mounts of modern animals. These have been collected around the world since 1830 (413-542-2165, www.amherst.edu/~pratt/).

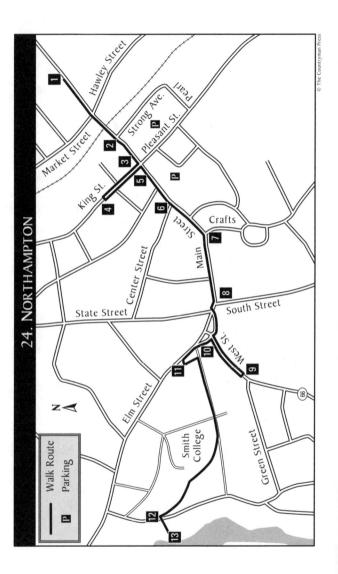

24. NORTHAMPTON

Walk Route
P Parking

N

1
Hawley Street
Market Street
2
3
Strong Ave.
Pearl
P
Pleasant St.
King St.
5
4
P
6
Center Street
Main Street
Crafts
7
State Street
8
South Street
West St.
10
11
9
Elm Street
66
Smith College
Green Street
12
13

© The Countryman Press

24·Northampton

Directions: *By car:* Take I-90, the Massachusetts Turnpike, west to exit 4, then I-91 north to exit 18. Follow US 5 north and then MA 9 west. *By public transportation:* Peter Pan Bus Lines (1-800-343-9999, www.peterpanbus. com) and Vermont Transit (1-800-642-3133, www.vermonttransit.com) offer service to Northampton.

Located on the Connecticut River, the Indians called this place Nonotuck, the middle of the river. In 1654 English colonists renamed it Northampton after the English town.

Begin at the Historic Northampton Museum and Education Center (1), which has a collection of nearly fifty thousand objects. Clustered on a single property are the visitors center, museum, the Damon House (1813), the Parsons House (1730), the Shepherd House (1796), a barn, and the museum shop (413-584-6011, www.historic-northampton.org).

From the museum turn right and walk under the railroad bridge. (Be sure to look at the mural). The neoclassical, yellow brick Masonic Block (2), built in 1898, will be on the right. It is notable because a young lawyer named Calvin Coolidge had his office here on the second floor from 1898 to 1919. Coolidge was born in

Vermont and spent much of his adult life in Northampton. He was Northampton's mayor before being elected governor of Massachusetts. Later elected vice president, he was sworn in as president when Warren G. Harding died in 1923. He was subsequently elected president and served one full term, returning to Northampton in 1929. Silent Cal did not run for a second term as president.

Just a few steps farther at 51 Main Street the Smith Charities building (3) will be on the right. The charity was begun in 1845 and is still active today. The sandstone Renaissance Revival headquarters was built in 1865.

Turn right onto King Street. Wiggins Tavern (4) will be on the left. Built by Benjamin Wiggins in 1786, the tavern was moved here from Hopkinton, New Hampshire, timber by timber, in 1930. It is now an adjunct of the Hotel Northampton (1927). The hotel lobby has a fine collection of old paintings and portraits, antiques, early American toys, and period pieces (413-584-3100, www.hotelnorthampton.com).

Return to Main Street. The granite and brownstone Court House (5) was built in 1885. A Romanesque Revival building, it was inspired by the works of H. H. Richardson. The first town meetinghouse was built on this site in the mid-1600s. Later, the courthouse was the scene of an episode in Shay's Rebellion (1786). Inside is a mural, *Work, Religion, Education,* painted by Alfred Crimini as a WPA project in the 1930s. The courthouse also has a bell that was cast in Paul Revere's foundry.

The First Church (6) will be next on the right. This, the fifth church to stand on this site, is a brownstone Victorian High Gothic Revival design by Peabody and

Stearns (1877). Opposite the church, along Main Street, is the old Shop Row, which includes the multilevel Forbes Marketplace.

Continue to walk along Main Street. Victorian-era shops are on the right, and City Hall (7) is on the left. A curious mix of Gothic, Norman, and Tudor styles, it was designed by William Fenno Pratt in 1859. The Greek Revival Unitarian Church stands next to City Hall. Built in 1903, it is a reproduction of an 1825 church that stood on the site and was destroyed by fire. Beyond the church is the red brick Memorial Hall, which is topped with a mansard roof.

The Academy of Music (8) is at the next corner. A neo-classical design, it is an 1891 work of William Brocklesby, is the oldest municipal theater in the country, and has hosted many notable performers in its long history. Between the Academy of Music and Memorial Hall is Pulaski Park, named in honor of the Polish hero of the American Revolution.

Cross South Street. The building on the left with bas reliefs of children's faces was a school until the 1980s. Beyond the Baptist Church, around the bend on West Street, is the Forbes Library (9). Another William Brocklesby design, the Romanesque Revival granite and brownstone building was completed in 1894. Step inside and see the Calvin Coolidge Memorial Room and exhibits of local memorabilia.

The tour continues on the campus of Smith College (10). Walk through the wrought-iron entry gates. Called the Grecourt Gates, they are the copy of those at the Chateau Robecourt in Grecourt, France. College Hall is before you. The collegiate Gothic building was designed by Peabody and Stearns. When it was dedicated in 1875 it housed all of Smith College. Just four years earlier Sophia Smith left a bequest of $400,000 to found an all-women's college. Today the campus covers 125 acres and has a student population of over 2,500.

To the right of College Hall is the Smith Museum of Art (11), which has recently undergone a $35 million renovation and expansion program culminating with a reopening in spring 2003. On view is an outstanding collection of paintings, sculpture, and works on paper. American, European, African, Asian, Native American, ancient, and contemporary works are in the permanent collection. Special exhibits are mounted (413- 585-2760, www.smith.edu/artmuseum).

The next stop is the Lyman Conservatory (12). To get there take the path between College Hall and the museum. After passing Neilson Library take the path that veers to the right. The conservatory, begun in 1894, has grown to include fern and succulent houses, covering many ranges, seasons, and continents. The conservatory is an idyllic escape in winter, the adjacent gardens and arboretum equally inviting in warmer seasons (413-585-2740, www.smith.edu).

Behind the conservatory, across College Avenue, is Paradise Pond (13). The famed 19th-century singer Jenny Lind, the Swedish Nightingale, was so impressed with the pond's beauty she declared, "This surely must be the Paradise of America."

25 · Deerfield

Directions: *By car:* Take I-90, the Massachusetts Turnpike, west to exit 4, then I-91 north to exit 24. Take US 5/MA 10 north and follow the signs to Old Deerfield. *By public transportation:* Peter Pan Bus Lines (1-800-343-9999, www.peterpanbus.com) offers service to Deerfield.

When Deerfield was founded in 1669, it was a frontier town at the far northwestern reach of New England. Caught in the French and Indian War, it was twice devastated by attacks: in 1675 at the Bloody Brook Massacre and again in 1704 at the Deerfield Raid, when the town was torched and burned. After the Treaty of Paris was signed in 1763, settlers began to rebuild. Deerfield Academy, a preparatory school, was founded in 1797. The Street, Deerfield's mile-long main street, is lined with preserved, restored, and rebuilt 17th-, 18th-, and 19th-century homes and public buildings, many of which are open to visitors. Most of the sites on this walking tour are opened to the public by Historic Deerfield, an organization founded by Mr. and Mrs. Henry N. Flynt in 1952 (413-774-5581, www.historic-deerfield.org).

Begin with a visit to Hall Tavern Information Center (1). Built 1765 in Claremont, Massachusetts, the tavern was moved to this site in 1949.

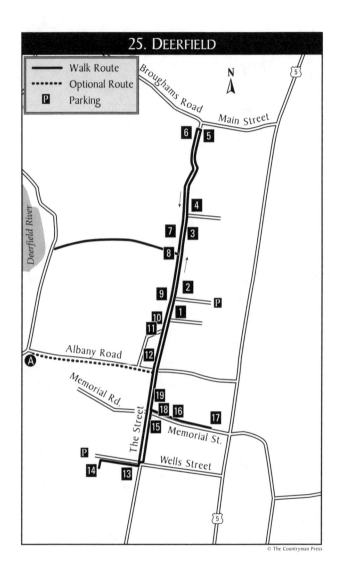

25. DEERFIELD

Walk Route
Optional Route
P Parking

N

Broughams Road

Main Street

Deerfield River

Albany Road

A

Memorial Rd.

The Street

Memorial St.

Wells Street

P

5

5

© The Countryman Press

After leaving the tavern turn right. The Stebbins House (2), a red brick Federal house built in 1799, will be on the right. Walk along The Street and past the Liberty Pole, the orchard, the Pink House (1797), and the Bement School (1925—a primary boarding and day school). Stop at the Allen House (3), built in 1725, home of Historic Deerfield founders Henry and Helen Flynt. Furnished with Colonial antiques, it is open to visitors.

Resume your walk along The Street. On the right is the gambrel-roofed Clesson House (4), which was built in 1814 and now houses the Henry N. Flynt Silver and Metalware collection. Just next door on the side street is the Helen Geier Flynt Textile Museum, housed in an 1872 barn.

Walk along The Street past the Hinsdale and Anne Williams House (1816). The next house is the red brick Federal Wright House (5), built in 1825, which exhibits the Cluett Collection of Chinese Export Porcelain and American Furniture and Clocks.

Cross the street to gambrel-roofed Ashley House (6). Built in 1730 and expanded in 1757, this was once home to Reverend Jonathan Ashley and was the first of the Deerfield houses to be opened to the public, in 1948.

Reverse direction and walk south on The Street. The next house on the right will be the Sheldon-Hawks House (c. 1743). Continue past several private homes built in Colonial, Colonial Revival, and Italianate styles, and stop at the Indian House Memorial (7). Built in 1929, it is a reproduction of an earlier house that stood on the site and had survived the French and Indian attack in 1704. The log building in back of the memo-

Wright House

rial is the 18th-century Bloody Brook Tavern. The memorial, tavern, and a children's museum are used for educational programs by the Pocumtuck Valley Memorial Association (413-774-3768, ext. 2, www.deerfield-ma.org).

Unique on this tour is the next house, a Gothic

Revival "cottage" built in 1848 for the Reverend John Farwell Moors.

Not to be missed is the Channing Blake Meadow Walk (8) which starts just beyond the Moors House and ends along the banks of the Deerfield River. Along the way you will see not only a working farm with livestock, but also distant views of the Berkshire foothills.

After the meadow walk return to The Street, turn right, and resume your walk south. The next stop is the Deerfield Inn (9), opened in 1884. Restored after a 1979 fire, the inn is open to the public for fine dining and accommodations. Next door is a former general store, which today serves Historic Deerfield as its museum store and bookshop.

Next you'll see the post office (10), built in 1952 to replicate Deerfield's third meetinghouse, which was built in 1728. The First Church of Deerfield (11) is a Federal-style building constructed in 1824. Weekly services are held in the Brick Church.

The town common (12) has historical markers that retell the story of the French and Indian attack of 1704. Note the statue that commemorates not only Civil War casualties, but also the bravery of Deerfield's settlers during the 1704 siege. The sycamore tree at the corner of Albany Road is Deerfield's oldest tree, growing before the first English settlers arrived in 1669. This is the threshold of Deerfield Academy, a secondary boarding school that has been very much a part of Deerfield since the school's founding in 1797. At first a school for boys, the academy is now coeducational.

Option A: The Burial Ground is farther down Albany Road. An Indian burial ground, it was later used by the colonists. The earliest stones date to the 1690s.

As you walk along The Street the next house open to visitors is the Dwight House (13). Built in Springfield about 1725, the house was moved here in the 1950s. The Flynt Center of Early New England Life (14) is behind the Dwight House. Opened in 1997, the 27,000-square-foot building is Historic Deerfield's "attic," where thousands of pieces of furniture and artifacts are in storage—yet on display for visitors to view. The center also mounts changing special exhibits.

After visiting the Flynt Center return to The Street, reverse direction, and walk north, back toward the common. Stop at the Wells-Thorn House (15) at the corner of Memorial Street. An 18th-century house, it was painted a light blue the following century. Its period rooms are furnished with the very best decorative arts available in Deerfield from 1725 to 1850.

Turn right onto Memorial Street. The White Church, or Orthodox Congregational Church (16), was built in 1838 following a split among the town's Congregationalists. The Unitarians retained the use of the First Church; the Trinitarians built this one. Today the White Church serves as a community center and an auditorium. The town office (1895) and Town Hall (1841, 1878) are next on Memorial Street.

The Memorial Hall Museum (17), housed in a 1798 Benjamin Asher building, was opened in 1880 by the Pocumtuck Valley Memorial Association. It is said to be the first American museum to display period rooms (413-774-3768, ext. 2, www.deerfield-ma.org). The Memorial Libraries are next door.

Return to The Street. Turn right. The Barnard Tavern (18), which dates to 1795, is on your right. The Frary House (19), built about 1750, is next. Restored by

Charlotte Alice Baker in 1892, it is filed with antique furniture, baskets, needlework, and ironware.

Walk past the three Deerfield Academy Colonial Revival dormitories, built in the 1950s. The Headmaster's House, also known as the Joseph Barnard house, built 1772, is just beyond. You have come full circle with your return to Hall Tavern, completing the walking tour of Historic Deerfield.

26 · Stockbridge

Directions: *By car:* Take I-90, the Massachusetts Turnpike, west to exit 2. Then take MA 102 south to Stockbridge. *By public transportation:* Bonanza Bus Lines (1-888-751-8800, www.bonanzabus.com) offers service to Stockbridge.

This picture postcard town set along the banks of the Housatonic River in the Berkshire Hills was established by Englishmen in 1734 as a Christian mission to the local Indians. The missionaries called it Indian Town. It was incorporated and renamed for Stockbridge, in Hampshire, England, in 1739. In the 19th and 20th centuries the town became a haven for writers and artists. Nathaniel Hawthorne lived here, as did sculptor Daniel Chester French. Perhaps the town's best-known resident was Norman Rockwell, who immortalized its citizens and Main Street in his paintings.

Your walking tour begins at Stockbridge's town green (1) on Main Street. Note the Children's Chime Tower (1878) and the Greek Revival Town Hall. The Congregational Church building dates to 1824, though the congregation first gathered in 1739. Just west of the church and tower, on the south side of Main Street, is a stone obelisk that marks the site of the Indian burial ground.

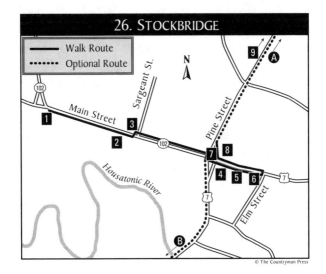

26. STOCKBRIDGE

— Walk Route
•••••• Optional Route

Reverse direction. Walk along Main Street toward the town center. The Merwin House (2), also known as Tranquillity, is on the right at number 14. The oldest part of this late Federal house was built in 1825. A shingle-style ell was added in 1900, doubling the buidling's size. Furnished with European and American period pieces, Merwin House is opened to the public by the Society for the Preservation of New England Antiquities (413-298-4703, www.spnea.org).

Still on Main Street, you can see the Mission House (3) opposite Tranquility. John Sergeant was the first Christian missionary in this area. In 1739 he built this house for his wife, Abigail. The house and it colonial gardens are open for tours by the Trustees of Reservations (413-298-3239, www.thetrustees.org).

As you continue along Main Street the Red Lion Inn (4) will be on the right just beyond the Cat and Dog

Fountain (1862). The first Red Lion Inn stood here in 1773. The present inn was built in 1897. If it looks familiar, it may be that you recognize the facade from some of Norman Rockwell's paintings. Step inside and look around. The public rooms are furnished with many antiques; a collection of colonial-era china is on display. Presidents William McKinley, Theodore and Franklin Roosevelt, Grover Cleveland, and Calvin Coolidge have stayed here, as have other notables, including Nathaniel Hawthorne, Henry Wadsworth Longfellow, Thornton Wilder, and John Wayne.

Just two doors down from the inn is the red brick Town Office (5), built in 1884. Note the stepped roof, which is reminiscent of Dutch Colonial architecture. Norman Rockwell's *The Marriage License* was painted inside this building.

The Stockbridge Library (6) is on the next corner. Visit the Historical Room—a museum and research library.

From the library cross Main Street and reverse direction, returning to Pine Street. The Soldiers Monument (7), erected in 1866, stands at the intersection of Main and Pine Streets. St. Paul's Episcopal Church (8) was built in 1884 of local limestone. The architect was the famous Charles F. McKim. The interior of this Norman Revival church has sculpture by Augustus Saint-Gaudens and Daniel Chester French—two of America's best-known and finest 19th-century sculptors. The baptistry was designed by Stanford White; Louis Comfort Tiffany designed and constructed the stained-glass windows. Norman Rockwell's funeral took place here (413-298-4913).

From St. Paul's, walk up Pine Street and then

Prospect Hill Road about ½ mile. Naumkeag (9) will be on the left. Designed by Stanford White in 1885, Naumkeag was the home of Joseph Hodges Choate (1832–1917), one-time ambassador to the Court of St. James. The house remains as Choate left it, decorated with antique furniture, tapestries, oriental rugs, and an outstanding collection of Chinese export porcelain. The Fletcher Steele gardens are thought to be among America's finest. Naumkeag is open to visitors by the Trustees of Reservations (413-298-3239, www.thetrustees.org).

Option A: Across the street from Naumkeag's entrance is the National Shrine of the Divine Mercy. The granite for the church was brought from the Westinghouse estate in Lenox. The Romanesque Revival church's interior is fitted with carved wood and embellished with murals and stained-glass windows. Beyond the church are fields, woods, and a grotto. Built by Polish émigrés, the shrine is internationally known and welcomes all visitors. A shop is on the premises (413-298-3931, www.marian.org).

Option B: For a country walk farther afield, explore the Ice Glen. Start at the Red Lion Inn and walk south several blocks on Route 7. Make a left on Park Street (where there is parking) and cross the footbridge spanning the Housatonic River. Follow the trails to Laura's Tower. Climb the tower and enjoy the panoramic views of three states: Massachusetts, Vermont, and New York.

27 · Williamstown

Directions: *By car:* Take I-90, the Massachusetts Turnpike, west to exit 2. Then take US 20 north to US 7, and follow it north to Williamstown. *By public transportation:* Two bus companies service Williamstown: Bonanza Bus Lines (1-888-751-8800, www.bonanzabus.com) and Vermont Transit (1-800-642-3133, www.vermonttransit.com).

This colonial settlement was first known as West Hoosac (1753). In 1765 Col. Ephraim Williams bequeathed a sum of money for a "free school." Both town and school (Williams College, founded in 1793) were renamed in honor of their benefactor.

Start this tour of Williamstown at Field Park (1), at the intersection of MA 2 and US 7. Originally, Williamstown's green was a common grazing field and ran the length of Main Street. In 1878 Cyrus Fields created the present park. The first and second meetinghouses, built in 1768 and 1798, stood on this site. Note the 1753 house, constructed during Williamstown's bicentennial in 1953. It is a reproduction of a regulation house built by British settlers in this area.

Next visit the House of Local History (2), located at the David and Joyce Milne Public Library just across the street from Field Park at 1095 Main Street (413-458-

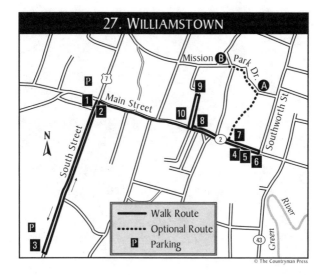

27. WILLIAMSTOWN

Mission **B** Park Dr. **A**

Main Street

South Street

Southworth St.

River

Green

— Walk Route
••••• Optional Route
P Parking

© The Countryman Press

2160, www.williamstown.net/house_of_local_history.htm).

From the House of Local History turn left onto Main Street and then left again onto South Street. It is about 1 mile down South Street to the Sterling and Francine Clark Art Institute (3), which is both a museum and a center for higher education and research. It was chartered by the Singer Sewing Machine heir Robert Sterling Clark and his wife Francine. The classical revival white marble building (1955) sits in a bucolic setting in the countryside. A wing designed by Pietro Belluschi was added in 1973. The museum's outstanding collection includes French Impressionist and post-Impressionist art (Renoir, Monet, Degas, Manet, Gauguin), American art (Homer, Sargent, Remington, Cassatt), European paintings spanning more than five centuries (Ruisdael, Millet, Corot, Tiepolo, Fragonard, David,

Main Street, Williamstown

Turner, Goya), and American and European decorative arts. Following a visit to the galleries you may want to follow the institute's Pasture Loop, which meanders through the surrounding woodlands and fields, and is punctuated with views of the town, the Greylock Range, and Vermont. A map of the loop is available at the museum's information desk (413-458-2303, www.clarkart.edu).

After visiting the Clark Institute, retrace your steps to Field Park. From South Street turn right onto Main Street. Many of the sites along Main Street are part of the Williams College campus. The estate of Col. Ephraim Williams funded the opening of the English Free School and Academy, which was replaced by Williams College in 1793. Just ahead on the right you'll see West College. Dating to 1791, it has housed the Free School, the Academy, and College.

Cross Spring Street to the Dolomite Building. The Stone Chapel and Alumni Hall are on the right. The brick octagonal building just beyond Alumni Hall is Lawrence Hall. Built to house the College Library in 1846, this has been the Williams College Museum of Art (4) since 1926. The museum's collection includes twelve thousand artworks representing a broad spectrum of cultures and periods. A highlight is the largest single collection, over four hundred pieces, of works by brothers Maurice and Charles Prendergast (413-597-2429, www.williams.edu/scma/).

Next door to the museum is East College (5). The present building (1841) replaces an earlier, 1797 building that was destroyed by fire.

Next is the Hopkins Observatory and Mehlin Museum of Astronomy (6). Built in 1836, this is the oldest working observatory in America. There are exhibits on the history of astronomy, plus planetarium shows and telescopes that visitors can use (413-597-2188, www.williams.edu/astronomy/hopkins/).

Reverse direction on Main Street. After crossing

Southworth Street, Griffin Hall (1828) will be on the right; beyond that is the Thompson Memorial Chapel (7). The tower of the limestone English Gothic Revival church, built in 1903, rises 120 feet. Most noteworthy perhaps is the stained-glass window in the south transept, dedicated to President James A. Garfield, who was a Williams College alumnus (class of 1856). The window was designed by John LaFarge and originally placed in the Old Stone Chapel across Main Street.

Option A: The Chapin Library of Rare Books is in Stetson Hall behind Thompson Memorial Chapel. On permanent display are original American Revolution–era documents, including the Declaration of Independence, the U.S. Constitution, the Bill of Rights, and George Washington's copy of *The Federalist Papers.* Additionally, there are changing exhibits of manuscripts and books from the 9th through the 20th centuries.

Option B: The Haystack Monument is located in Mission Park northwest of Chapin Library. In an 1806 event a group of five students met on the site to pray for missions. A storm brewed and all five sought shelter in a nearby haystack. This led to the founding of the first American Protestant Foreign Mission. The 12-foot-high granite monument, dedicated in 1867, is inscribed "The Field is the World."

The First Congregational Church (8) is at the corner of Main Street and Chapin Hall Drive. Field Park was the site of the congregation's first two meetinghouses. When the second was destroyed by fire in 1866 it was replaced with this church. At first this was a red brick Romanesque Revival building, but in 1914 the outside of the church was enveloped in white clapboard, creating the classical exterior you see today.

Set back from Main Street, at the far side of a lawn, is Chapin Hall (9), designed by the firm of Cram and Ferguson. Its portico has a row of massive Corinthian columns. Step inside and see the large Burmese teak pillars and carved woodwork.

Resume your walk on Main Street. The Sloan House (10), at number 936, is a Federal house built in 1802. It has been the Williams College Presidents House since 1858. You have come full circle and are standing near the starting point of this tour.

III. Rhode Island

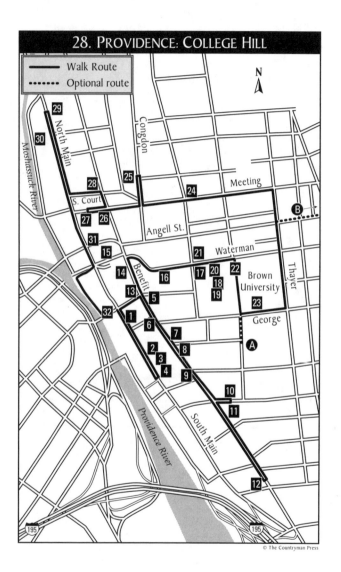

28. PROVIDENCE: COLLEGE HILL

Walk Route
Optional route

N

Moshassuck River

29 North Main
30

Congdon

28 S. Court
25
24 Meeting

B

27 26
31
Angell St.
15
14 Benefit
13
21 Waterman
16
17
20 22
18
19 Brown University
5
32
1
6
23
7 George
2
3
8 A
4
9
10
11
12 South Main

Providence River

195 195

© The Countryman Press

28 · Providence: College Hill

Directions: *By car:* Take I-95 south to exit 22. Follow Memorial Boulevard east and cross the Providence River on College Street to the courthouse. *By public transportation:* There are three options: Bonanza Bus Line (1-888-751-8800, www.bonanzabus.com), MBTA Commuter Rail (1-800-392-6100, www.mbta.com), or AMTRAK (1-800-USA-RAIL, www.amtrak.com).

Roger Williams founded Providence in 1636. A minister, he was exiled from Plymouth Colony because of religious disagreements. Accompanied by five compatriots, he canoed along the Moshassuck River and settled on what is now called College Hill. Purchasing land from the Indian Chiefs Miantonomi and Cononicus, he named the settlement for "God's merciful providence" which had led him to this site.

The settlement grew along Towne Street (today's North and South Main Streets), parallel to the banks of the Providence River. Houses were built on Towne Street. Long, narrow lots extended up the hill and were used as gardens, livestock pens, and family burial plots. As the city and waterfront grew Towne Street became congested. In 1757 Back Street, at the back of Towne Street's housing lots, was developed; it was later renamed Benefit Street as it benefited all. From the late 18th century and through the 19th, Benefit Street was Providence's most fashionable address. Following a period of decline, it was revitalized in the late 20th century, largely through the efforts of the Providence Preservation Society.

This walking tour begins, appropriately, where Providence began: along the banks of the river and within sight of Towne Street, now South Main Street. The Providence County Courthouse (1), completed in 1933, was the work of local architects Jackson, Robertson, and Adads. A modern building, its design incorporates many Georgian Revival details. The red brick block just to the right of the courthouse was built in the mid-1800s as shops and apartments. More notable, perhaps, is the building that is next on the right. The Joseph Brown House (2), at 50 South Main, was built in 1774 by gentleman architect Joseph Brown, some of whose works are featured later on this walk. The house stands on the site of the Field Garrison House, where Roger Williams and his followers gathered in 1676 when the Indians attacked and burned the town. Note the curved, baroque gabled roof. The builder's brothers, John and Moses Brown, converted the house for use as the Providence Bank in 1791.

The large granite building to the right is the Old Stone Bank (3). Built for the Providence Institution for Savings in 1854, the templelike Greek Revival bank was enlarged and topped with its distinctive, shallow, gilded copper dome in 1898.

The next house on the right is the Benoni Cooke House (4), at 110 South Main. This is one of a pair of Federal houses built here in 1828 and designed by John

Holden Green. The second house was demolished in the 1890s when the Old Stone Bank was expanded.

You are about to ascend College Hill. But first, a few words about the monuments in the surrounding park: The tall, needlelike monument was dedicated in 1929 as the city's World War I memorial. Close by are the Korean War memorial, designed by Robert Shure and constructed in 1999, and a work of art entitled *Welded Iron Sculpture,* created by de Almeida in 1985.

Walk up College Street, which is just to the left of the courthouse. Benefit Street is one block up. The Providence Athenaeum (5) is the granite Greek Revival building in front of you. Established in 1753 as the Providence Library Company, this is the oldest library in the city and one of the oldest in the nation. Resembling a Doric temple, the building was completed in 1838 using designs by the great Philadelphia architect William Stickland. (This is Stickland's only work in New England.) Wings were added in 1910 (Norman Isham, architect) and in 1979 (Warren Platner, architect). The Romanesque fountain was added at street level in 1873. It is flanked by Greek Revival wrought-iron fences that date to the 1830s. The athenaeum houses an impressive library and art collection, which has been used by the likes of Edgar Allan Poe, John James Audubon, Ralph Waldo Emerson, and Henry Wadsworth Longfellow. It is open to the public (401-421-6970, www.providenceathenaeum.org).

To the right of the atheneum you'll see a row of Greek Revival houses, at numbers 257 through 263, built in the early 19th century. A similar row of houses is across the street at numbers 270 through 276.

The small house (6) at the corner of Hopkins Street

was built about 1707, with an addition in 1743. This was the home of Stephen Hopkins, a signer of the Declaration of Independence and governor of Rhode Island for ten terms. George Washington slept here. The house was restored by architect Norman Isham, who is well-known for his extensive restoration work in Colonial Williamsburg. Maintained by the Rhode Island chapter of the National Society of the Colonial Dames of America, the house is open to the public by written request (President, Governor Stephen Hopkins House Committee, 15 Hopkins Street, Providence, RI 02903).

Continue along Benefit Street. On the left, at number 6 Benevolent Street, is the private Hope Club (7). Founded in 1875, the clubhouse was built in 1886 and is believed to be the oldest structure in America built specifically as a clubhouse.

The First Unitarian Church (8) on the left (1816) was designed by local architect John Holden Greene. The white stone used here was quarried in Johnston, Rhode Island. Greene's design combines classical and Gothic decorative elements. For example, note the two-story windows, which are rounded at the tops, while the window mullions are Gothic. The tower, somewhat reminiscent of that at St. Martin-in-the-Fields in Trafalgar Square, London, holds the largest bell ever cast by Paul Revere. This is considered Greene's masterpiece. Later you will see another of his church designs (401-421-7970, www.firstunitarianprov.org).

Walk to the corner of Benefit and Planet Streets. On the right, at number 314, is General Ambrose Burnside's house (9), built in 1866 in the French Second Empire style. Burnside was a Civial War general, Rhode Island governor, and U.S. Senator. The distinctive whiskers that

The Providence River and College Hill

grew down the sides of his face were imitated by others and became known as sideburns.

Turn left onto Power Street and on the left you'll see the John Brown House (10), constructed between the years 1785 and 1788. Brown was a prosperous merchant. His brother Joseph, whose house you saw at the beginning of this tour, designed this mansion. It was filled with the finest furnishings money could buy. John Quincy Adams said this was "the most magnificent and elegant private mansion that I have ever seen on this continent." Today it is opened for tours by the Rhode Island Historical Society (401-331-8575, www.rihs.org).

The Joseph Nightingale House (11) is at 357 Benefit Street between Power and Williams Streets. Built in 1792, this was lived in by members of the Brown family from 1814 through 1985. It is now the John Nicholas Brown Center for the Study of American Civilization and is open to the public by appointment (401-863-1000, www.brown.edu/administration/george_st).

Note the Barker Playhouse (12) at the corner of Benefit and Transit Streets, which was built in 1840 as St. Stephen's Church. Later on this tour is the parish's second church.

There is a small cemetery next to the theater. When Benefit Street was developed the graves in the lots were moved to North Burial Ground. This is the sole remaining cemetery on the street.

Across the street at 389 Benefit is an Italian palazzo–style brownstone house that was built in 1853. Across John Street stands a second "palazzo," at number 383.

Going back one century, the house at 368 Benefit Street was built in 1795. As you walk the length of Benefit you will see that many of the houses have plaques that identify the builder and the building date. Many of the labels are there through the sponsorship of the Providence Preservation Society.

Retrace your steps to the corner of Benefit and College Streets and cross College Street. On the left, at 226 Benefit, is a large brownstone Romanesque building. For many years this was Central Church, whose congregation now worships on Angell Street. Built in 1853, its spires were destroyed by the 1938 hurricane. This is now Memorial Hall (13), a facility of the Rhode Island School of Design (RISD). Founded in 1877, RISD (pronounced *riz*-dee) is a premier educational institution granting degrees in the fine arts, architecture, and design.

Just a few steps from Memorial Hall is the Rhode Island School of Design Museum of Art (14). The 18th-century Pendleton House contains the museum's American furniture and decorative arts collection. Adjacent wings have been added since 1926 and house collections of paintings, sculpture, ancient art, Asian art, costumes and textiles, prints, drawings, photographs, and decorative arts. The museum has more than 85,000 works in its collection. At the time of this writing a building expansion is planned (401-454-6500, www.risd.edu). The sculpture *Orpheus Ascending* (1963), by Gilbert Franklin, sits in Frazier Terrace opposite the museum.

Proceed to the corner of Benefit and Waterman Streets. Before you is the First Baptist Church in America (15). Founded by Roger Williams and his companions in 1638, the present church building was completed in 1775. Another Joseph Brown design, the architect borrowed from the work of Englishman James Gibbs; its spire is another St. Martin-in-the-Fields copy. The result is a New England meetinghouse with Georgian elements. This was the largest church in colonial America, seating 1,400 (about one-third of the city's population at that time). Brown University uses the church "for the public worship of Almighty God and also for holding Commencement in." To see the inside enter through the ground-floor door on the Waterman Street side (401-454-3418).

After seeing the church walk up the hill on Waterman Street, a steep climb. Note the large concrete building on the right. This is the List Art Center (16), designed by Philip Johnson and constructed in 1971. The center's Bell Gallery presents major art exhibitions (401-863-2932, www.brown.edu).

When you reach the corner of Waterman and Prospect Streets stop, rest a bit, and note the array of buildings before you, which are on Brown University's campus. The school began in 1764 as the College of

Rhode Island. In 1894 Nicholas Brown made an endowment and the college was renamed in his honor. Today the university has almost seven thousand students and 550 full-time faculty members. The campus covers 142 acres (401863-1000, www.brown.edu).

A Brown landmark, the Carrie Tower (17), is in front of you. To the right note the Greek Revival Manning Hall (18). Built in 1833 and based on Sicilian prototypes, the upper level of the hall houses a chapel. To the right of Manning is University Hall (19), Brown's oldest building. Another Joseph Brown design, this Georgian building was completed in 1771. During the Revolution American and French troops used it as a barracks. To the left of Manning Hall is Federal-style Hope College (20), Brown's second-oldest building (1822). Hope College was named after Nicholas Brown's sister.

Look further to your left, kitty-corner across Waterman and Prospect Streets. The Victorian High Gothic building is Robinson Hall (21), built in 1875 as a library. The floor plan was one used at many libraries: multi-level stacks surrounding a large, central reading room. Continue up Waterman Street. Brown Street will be on the left. Opposite Brown Street, the Arch is on your right. Walk under the Arch (22) and the length of the college green. On the left is the Salomon Center and Rogers Hall (23), built in 1862, then Sayles Hall (1881). Next is the Richardsonian Romanesque Wilson Hall (1891). The last building on the left is the John Carter Brown Library (1904). Built in the beaux-arts style, the library's exterior is Indiana limestone. There are two outdoor sculptures along the way: Henry Moore's *Bridge-Prop* (1963), and Eli Harvey's bear, *Bruno* (1923).

When you leave the college green you will be on George Street.

Option A: The Maryann Brown Memorial is just steps away at 21 Brown Street (straight ahead as you leave the green). The memorial houses two galleries with dozens of paintings and Brown family memorabilia (401-863-1994).

With your back to the college green turn left and walk up George Street. St. Stephen's Church (23) will be on your left. Founded in 1837, the present Episcopal church was designed by Richard Upjohn in 1862 and is an example of middle pointed (or decorated) English Gothic Revival architecture. A brochure available in the narthex describes the church's decorative arts and appointments (401-421-6702, www.sstephens.org). St. Stephen's first church, seen earlier on the tour, is on Benefit Street.

The next corner will be the intersection of George and Thayer Streets. Turn left onto Thayer Street and walk straight to Meeting Street. There are many eateries along this stretch.

Option B: The Governor Henry Lippitt House Museum, a high Italianate villa, is "one of the most complete, authentic, and intact Victorian houses in the country," according to the *New York Times.* To reach the house make a right from Thayer Street onto Angell Street and walk two blocks to 199 Hope Street (401-453-0688).

When you reach the corner of Thayer and Meeting Streets turn left onto Meeting and begin your descent of College Hill. At Meeting and Prospect Streets you'll see the domed, Renaissance Revival First Church of Christ Scientist (24). Continue downhill on Meeting

Street and turn right onto Congdon Street. Prospect Terrace (25) will be on the left. Sit down and enjoy the unsurpassed view of the dome on the state capitol and the surrounding city. But you are not alone. The remains of Roger Williams are buried under his statue, which overlooks the city he founded in 1636. The statue was sculpted by Leo Friedlander in 1939. This is a favorite overlook, and many a scene for the television series *Providence* was filmed at Prospect Terrace.

Return to Meeting Street and resume your descent. Stop at the corner of Meeting and Benefit Streets and look at the Marine Corps Arsenal (26). Designed by Rhode Island architect Russell Warren in 1840, this is a Gothic Revival fortress complete with lookout towers.

Your next stop will be the John Carter House (27), built in 1772, at 21 Meeting Street. This is also known as Shakespeare's Head. In colonial times a pole, topped with a carving of the author's head, stood here as a shop sign. Across the way, at 24 Meeting Street, you'll see the Brick School House (1769). Today both the schoolhouse and Shakespeare's Head are occupied by Providence Preservation Society offices.

Return to Benefit Street. Turn left, and on the left will be the Old State House (28). Built in 1762, this was one of five capitol buildings in Rhode Island at that time; there was one capitol building in each of the state's counties. This is a copy of the English baroque Old Colony House built in Newport. Since colonial days there have been several additions and renovations to the Old State House. The Old Senate Chamber has been restored to look as it did in 1762. It was here that Rhode Island declared its independence from Great Britain on May 4, 1776—two months before the signing of the

Declaration of Independence. George Washington, Thomas Jefferson, and the Marquis de Lafayette were all lavishly entertained in the Old State House.

Walk around the Old State House to the side opposite Benefit Street. Walk to North Main Street and the foot of the Parade, the long, narrow park. With your back to the Old State House turn right and walk along North Main Street to the Cathedral of St. John (29). This is said to be the oldest Episcopal Cathedral in the United States. The congregation was founded in 1722, when the cornerstone for the King's Church was laid by a small community of local Anglicans. After the Revolution, in 1794, King's Church was renamed St. John's Church. In 1810, John Holden Greene designed the present building—a Georgian church with Gothic details. Additions were made in 1868 and in 1905. St. John's was elevated to the status of a cathedral in 1929 (401-331-4622, www.cathstj@episcopalri.org).

The Roger Williams National Memorial (30) is across North Main Street. On this, the site of Roger Williams' 1636 settlement, is a visitors center with exhibits. The memorial is a National Park Service site (401-521-7266, www.nps.gov/rowi).

Look across the way to the dome of the Rhode Island State House (1904).

Walk along North Main Street. When you reach the First Baptist Meeting House again, look up Thomas Street to the left of the church. The Fleur-de-Lys House (31) at 7 Thomas Street was built in 1885 for artist Sydney Burleigh. Its neighbor is the Providence Art Club at 11 Thomas Street. Built in 1791, the house was remodeled in 1886 and today is a clubhouse and art gallery.

At the corner of Main and Waterman Streets turn

right onto Waterman and then left at the river. Walk along the river; RISD will be on the left. Note the braziers in the river. During scheduled evening presentations the braziers are filled with burning logs by Waterfire Providence. The creation of artist Barnaby Evans, Waterfire Providence has been declared by the *Providence Journal-Bulletin* to be "the most popular work of art created in the capital city's 361-year history." For schedules and information call 401-272-3111 (www.waterfire.org).

Just before College Street, you'll see the Brick Market House (32) on the left at Market Square, built in 1773 and designed by Joseph Brown and Stephen Hopkins. Note the arches on the ground-floor level, which were originally opened to accommodate merchants' carts. Used for many purposes, it was the City Building before City Hall was completed in 1878. Today Brick Market House is used by RISD.

The tour ends here just steps away from the spot where it started.

29 · Providence: The Capitol and the City

Directions: *By car:* Take I-95 south to exit 22 and follow signs to the State House. *By public transportation:* Bonanza Bus Lines (1-888-751-8800, www.bonanzabus.com), MBTA Commuter Rail (1-800-392-6100, www.mbta.com), and AMTRAK (1-800-USA-RAIL, www.amtrak.com) all offer service to Providence.

Roger Williams founded Providence in 1636, and in 1663 King Charles II granted a charter to "Rhode Island and Providence Plantations." The state has retained the name, making the smallest state one with the longest name. Throughout most of the 19th century there was a statehouse in each of Rhode Island's five counties, the legislature meeting in each on a rotating basis. Elsewhere in this book walking tours will visit three of the old statehouses: in Providence, Newport, and Bristol. Providence has been Rhode Island's sole capital since 1900. This tour begins at the current State House (1).

While it is by no measure the largest of state capitol buildings, this is arguably one of the most beautiful. Designed by McKim, Mead, and White in the American Renaissance style, the State House was completed in

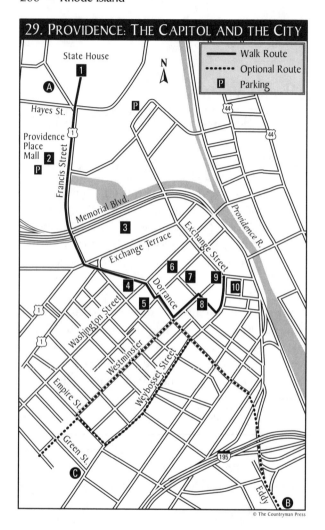

29. PROVIDENCE: THE CAPITOL AND THE CITY

State House

N

Walk Route
•••••• Optional Route
P Parking

A

Hayes St.

P

44

44

Providence Place Mall

2

P

Francis Street

1

1

Memorial Blvd.

3

Exchange Terrace

Exchange Street

Providence R.

6

7

9

Dorance

4

8

10

5

1

Washington Street

1

Westminster

Weybosset Street

Empire St.

Green St.

C

195

Eddy

B

© The Countryman Press

1904. The exterior is white Georgian marble. The most noteworthy feature is the massive dome—the fourth largest self-supporting dome in the world. (Only St.

Peter's Basilica in Rome, the Minnesota State Capitol, and the Taj Mahal have larger domes.) On top of the dome stands *The Independent Man*, with a spear in one hand and an anchor, Rhode Island's symbol, in the other. The statue was modeled by George Brewster in 1899. Inside the dome is a mural of Roger Williams and many of his contemporaries, both natives and colonists. The chambers are sumptuous. On display is the original Royal Charter of 1663 granted by King Charles II. A portrait of George Washington painted by Rhode Island native Gilbert Stuart hangs in the state reception room (401-222-2357).

Before leaving the capitol grounds and descending Smith Hill on Francis Street toward the city, note statues of two Rhode Islanders: Oliver Hazard Perry, the hero of the battle of Lake Erie during the War of 1812, and Gen. Nathanael Greene. Of interest to movie buffs: part of Steven Spielberg's *Amistad* was filmed on this lawn.

Option A: Once on Francis Street, to the right, on Hayes Street, you'll see the red brick and limestone Gloria Dei Lutheran Church. Note the Viking ship on the weathervane. This parish was founded by Swedes on 1890. Their distinctive church building was designed by the Swedish architect Martin Hedmark. His only church in America, Gloria Dei is a unique example of Swedish nationalist Romantic Revival architecture and is heavily influenced by the architecture of Swedish castles. In addition, the church has modern and art deco influences. A brochure describes the church and the symbolism used in its interior (401-421-5860).

Walk the length of Francis Street toward downcity. Providence Place Mall (2), completed in 1999, is on the right.

After crossing the Woonasquatucket River note the cluster of five Renaissance Revival brick buildings, with red trim, ahead on your left. This is Union Station (3), built in 1896. No longer a train station, it has been refurbished to house offices and restaurants. Since 1986 the Providence Station, on Smith Hill in the shadow of the State House, has served as the city's train depot.

Just ahead to the right are two recent additions to the city's landscape: the Westin Hotel and the Rhode Island Convention Center. The Biltmore Hotel (4), which dates to 1922, is beyond. The Biltmore's architects, Warren and Wetmore, also designed New York City's Biltmore, Pennsylvania, and Commodore Hotels. Its glass enclosed elevator whisks visitors to the top floor for a bird's-eye view of the city.

Walk from the Biltmore to City Hall (5). Built between 1874 and 1878, City Hall is an outstanding example of French Second Empire architecture. The grand entrance stairway has been the stage for many city gatherings and celebrations, including the annual First Night celebrations and the welcoming of the New England Patriots as Super Bowl heroes in 2002. Presidents Theodore Roosevelt and John F. Kennedy spoke from these steps.

Inside, the atrium, chambers, and corridors are painted and stenciled. From 1975 to 1990 the interior was meticulously restored to its original brilliance.

With your back to City Hall look at Kennedy Plaza (6). Created in 1848, this area was known as Exchange Place, and an earlier Union Station stood in the park on your left. Directly in front of you is the Soldiers and Sailors Monument (1871) and the City's Intermodular Transportation Center (2002). At the far end of the

The statue of Roger Williams loverlooks the city from Prospect Terrace

plaza, facing City Hall, is the Federal Building (1908). To your right are a row of office buildings. The tallest (7), an art deco, 26-story skyscraper constructed in 1928, was New England's tallest building when first built. Originally known as the Industrial Trust Company Building, it is now a part of the Fleet Center.

Immediately to your left is the Fleet Skating Center (401-331-5544, www.fleetskating.com). The park alongside contains the Bajnotti Fountain (1899) and a statue of General Ambrose Burnside, local hero, governor, U.S. senator, and the original wearer of sideburns.

Facing Kennedy Plaza, turn to your right and walk along Dorrance Street. Turn left onto Westminster Street. In the middle of the block on the right you'll see a magnificent granite Greek Revival temple. This is the Arcade (8), constructed in 1828 and designed by Russell Warren and James Bucklin. It is the oldest shopping mall in the United States. The six massive columns on the portico were quarried in Johnston, Rhode Island, and brought to this site by teams of oxen. Renovated in 1980, the Arcade's three levels are lit by skylights, and feature shops, eateries, and offices. Walk the length of the Arcade and exit at the opposite end of the building onto Weybosset Street.

Turn left on Weybosset Street and walk to the triangular intersection where Weybosset and Westminster Streets join (9). Look up and note the Turk's Head on the office building at the intersection, 7–17 Weybosset. Built in 1913, the office building stands on the site of a house that had a ship's head, a Turk, on its porch. Though the house is long gone, the intersection and office building have retained the name Turk's Head.

While facing the Turk's Head building look to your left. The granite three-story building on the left is another Federal Building (10). Built in 1855, this is an Italianate design. It has been a customs house, courthouse, and a post office. Look down the plaza on the left for a view across the Providence River to the dome of the Old Stone Bank (1854) and the spire of the First Unitarian Church (1816).

This is where your tour ends. Following are options.

Option B: It is a 10-minute walk from this spot to the Heritage Harbor Museum. Backtrack on Weybosset Street, past the Arcade, to the corner of Dorrance Street, and turn left onto Dorrance Street. Dorrance will veer to the right and merge with Eddy Street. The Heritage Harbor Museum (HHM) will be on the left. Housed in the former South Street Power Plant (1885) of the Narraganset Electric Company, HHM is Rhode Island's history museum and cultural center. The 250,000-square-foot museum is the joint effort of 19 historical and cultural organizations and is the only New England affiliate of the Smithsonian Institution. As such the Smithsonian makes long-term loans to HHM from its collection, and the museum hosts Smithsonian's traveling exhibits (401-751-7979, www.heritageharbor.org).

Davol Square is just beyond the museum. Dating to the 1880s, the former factory has been refurbished to house shops and offices.

Another museum in the neighborhood is the Providence Children's Museum. Look for the dragon perched on top of the museum's roof. A smaller museum, this is "a hands-on place where kids and grown-ups play and learn together" (401-273-KIDS, www.childrenmuseum.org).

Option C: Here is an opportunity to explore a former retail sales area, now designated as Providence's Art District. In addition to the district's many theaters, shops and department stores are being converted into galleries, artists' studios, and artists' housing. This walk through the Arts District also visits three architecturally significant churches.

Begin by retracing your steps down Weybosset Street and through the Arcade, emerging onto Westminster Street. Turn left and walk down Westminster Street. Grace Church is at the corner of Westminster and Matthewson Streets. The brownstone church was designed in 1845 by Richard Upjohn, who was the pre-eminent church architect in 19th-century America. One of his best-known works is Trinity Church, on Wall Street in New York City. The asymmetrical placement of the tower at the church's corner was a first. The bell tower has a peel of 16 bells cast in 1861. Inside, the outstanding collection of 15 stained-glass windows includes one by Tiffany. Installed over a period of a half-century, from 1875 to 1929, the windows are a textbook of

American stained-glass window history (401-331-3225; www.gracechurchprovidence.org).

After seeing Grace Church continue your walk along Westminster Street, cross Empire Street, and ascend the steps to the I. M. Pei–designed plaza at the entrance to the Cathedral of Saints Peter and Paul. The cathedral is the successor to the first Roman Catholic parish founded in Rhode Island in 1827. Rhode Island became an independent diocese in 1872, and in 1878 work was begun on the cathedral according to plans by Patrick C. Keely. Based in Brooklyn, Keely designed many Roman Catholic churches and several cathedrals. The rough-hewn sandstone facade combines Romanesque and German Gothic Revival styles. Outstanding features of the vast interior include the timber vaulted ceiling, 1886 Austrian stained-glass windows, and the main altar, which is carved from a single piece of French marble. The magnificent organ stands 36 feet high, and has four keyboards and more than 6,000 pipes (401-331-2434).

After seeing the cathedral (C), return to Empire Street, turn right, and then left onto Weybosset Street. On the right you'll see the Round Top Church, the Beneficent Congregational Church. This congregation had its roots in the First Congregational Church (now the First Unitarian Church) on College Hill at the corner of Benefit and Beneficent Streets. In 1743, during the Great Awakening, a group from the First Church separated, crossed the river, and built a church on this site. The present church was built in 1809, and is the oldest church building in Downcity Providence. In 1884 a truly noteworthy addition was made to the church interior: a 5,700-prism Austrian chandelier.

Remarkably, little else has changed on the inside of the church since its construction. The exterior, however, has seen some major modifications. In 1836 the architect James Bucklin transformed the facade, adding Greek Revival details which were so popular at that time. Note the cupola atop the "round top" or dome. It was modeled after the Lysicrates' Monument to Music, in Athens. This is a fitting symbol, as music has always been central to this congregation's mission and services (401-331-9844; www.beneficentchurch.org).

Walk along Weybosset Street. The Providence Performing Arts Center will be on the right. Built as Loew's State Theater in 1928, the theater was threatened with demolition 50 years later. A partnership of government and private interests not only saved the theater, but also facilitated its restoration and expansion of its facilities (401-421-ARTS; www.ppacri.org).

The collegiate quadrangle on the right is the nucleus of Johnson and Wales University. The campus was created in the 1980s on the site of the old Outlet Company Department Store. A four-year college and graduate school, Johnson and Wales offers degree programs in the culinary arts, the hospitality industry, and business (401-598-1000, www.jwu.edu).

30 · Newport: The Colonial City

Directions: *By car:* From MA 128 take MA 24 south through Fall River and into Rhode Island. Stay on MA/RI 24 until it ends, merging with RI 114. Take RI 114 south to Newport. Follow the signs to the Gateway Visitor Center. *By public transportation:* Direct service from Boston's South Station to Newport's Gateway Center is provided by Bonanza Bus Lines (1-888-751-8800, www.bonanzabus.com).

In 1524 the Italian navigator Giovanni da Verrazzano set sail for North America to explore the east coast of the continent for the King of France. Verrazzano moored his ship in Newport Harbor for about two weeks, noting that its native inhabitants were "the most beautiful people and the most civilized in customs that we have found in this navigation." A little more than a century later, in 1639, followers of Providence's Roger Williams sailed down Narragansett Bay and established this, a "New Port," where the bay and the ocean meet. Religious tolerance guaranteed by the Newport Compact attracted Baptists, Quakers, Sephardic Jews, and others. Their architectural heritage is evident on this tour.

Leave the Gateway Center (1). Next to the small train station across the street is the intersection of Bridge and

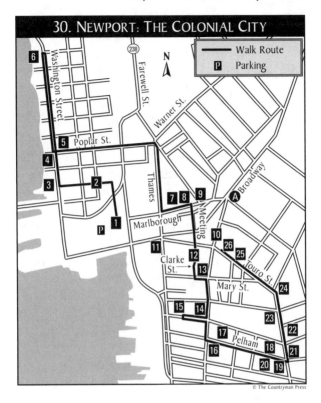

Third Streets (2). Begin by walking down Bridge Street with your back to the railroad station.

This is the colonial part of town known as The Point, so-called because a prominent pointed peninsula jutted into the harbor here. The Point was the first permanent Quaker neighborhood in America, predating those in Pennsylvania. The streets on the Point are either numbered or named after trees—a common Quaker practice to avoid exalting mortal men. Washington Street, however, is an exception.

Many of the houses along the tour have plaques. Bronze plaques indicate that the house is on the National Register of Historic Places. (The Point has been designated an Historic District by the National Register.) Other plaques are marked with a prominent OC. This stands for Operation Clapboard, a 1960s movement that encouraged the buying and restoration of historically significant houses. Still other plaques are marked NRF. These houses are the property of Doris Duke's Newport Restoration Foundation. Dozens of 18th- and 19th-century Newport houses have been restored by the NRF and are rented to tenants.

Stop at 77 Bridge Street, the former Pitt's Head Tavern. Built in 1726 and enlarged in 1744, the structure was originally on Washington Square. It was moved to this site in 1965 and is a private residence today.

Washington Street is at the end of Bridge Street. Cross Washington to Storer Park (3). Before you is Goat Island. Although no one is sure how Goat Island got its name, what is known is that in colonial times it was the site of a prison. This arrangement (and name, perhaps) may be a reflection of the biblical passage: "He shall separate them one from another, as a shepherd divideth his sheep from the goats: and he shall set the sheep on his right hand, but the goats on the left" (Matt. 25:32–33). In time Goat Island became the property of the navy, which operated a torpedo manufacturing station here during World War II. Later privatized and connected to Newport by the causeway on the left, today the island has a large luxury hotel, condominiums, and marinas.

Next to Storer Park is Hunter House (4), the first of several highlights on this tour. Construction began in

1748. Through the 18th century the house was enlarged, embellished, and furnished by a series of owners—the Nichols, the Wantons, and the Hunters. It was home to wealthy merchants, ambassadors, governors, and Admiral de Ternay—the Commander of French Naval Forces in America during the American Revolution. Note the carved pineapple over the door, a symbol of hospitality in colonial times. The interior is decorated with polychromed wood paneling, a boyhood painting by Rhode Island artist Gilbert Stuart, and several pieces by the Townsends and the Goddards, renowned Newport furniture makers. A small but beautiful 18th-century garden in back of the house overlooks the tranquil bay. Hunter House is opened to the public by the Preservation Society of Newport County (401-847-1000, www.newportmansions.org).

As you leave Hunter House turn to the left and walk along Washington Street. Gilbert Stuart's widow and his daughter (also an artist) lived for a time at the Capt. John Warren House at 62 Washington Street. Across the street, at Washington and Willow Streets, you'll see the only church on the Point—the Zabriskie Memorial Church of S. John the Evangelist (5). Founded in 1875 as a mission of Trinity Church, this building was completed in 1894. The architect was an Englishman, Frederick Clark Withers, and his design resembles many 13th-century English Gothic parish churches. The stained-glass window over the high altar was made by Hardman and Co. of London. The Blessed Sacrament Chapel, to the right of the nave, has exquisitely carved Gothic woodwork, all designed by the architect and medievalist Ralph Adams Cram, whose best-known work is the Cathedral of St. John the Divine in New

York City. S. John's sponsors an annual Celebration of British Cathedral Music when an English choir takes up residence here for a week, singing daily services (401-848-2561, www.saintjohns-newport.org).

Continue along Washington Street until you come to Battery Park (6), another small park overlooking the harbor and the site of old Fort Greene. Sit down and enjoy the view. To the right is the Newport-Pell Bridge, which was completed in 1969. Two miles long with 400-foot-tall towers, this is New England's longest suspension bridge. Immediately to your right, the cluster of white and granite buildings are the Naval War College (1883). Directly ahead is Rose Island, with its restored lighthouse. Visitors are welcome and the lighthouse is open to accommodate "guest keepers" (401-847-4242, www.roseislandlighthouse.org).

Retrace your steps along Washington Street. Just past S. John's turn left onto Poplar Street. The John Dennis House (c. 1740) sits at the corner of Washington and Poplar Streets. A couple of notable exceptions to Poplar's parade of colonial homes are number 63, an 1833 Greek Revival design, and number 57, an 1854 Victorian topped with a mansard roof. Cross America's Cup Avenue. Poplar Street ends at Thames Street, where you turn right. Thames Street dates to 1654 and as such is one of the oldest streets in America. John Stevens Shop, at 29 Thames Street, first opened in 1705. This stone-cutting and letter-design company is the oldest business in America continuously operating on its original site.

Turn left onto Marlborough Street, which also dates to 1654. St. Paul's Methodist Church (7), built in 1806, will be on your left. The church's interior is fitted with fine period woodwork and paneling (401-846-0966).

ROBERT J. REGALBUTO

The Redwood Library and Atheneum

Farther along Marlborough Street, on the left, is the red-clapboard White Horse Tavern (8). Built in 1673 and later enlarged, it is the oldest tavern in continuous operation in the nation (401-849-3600, www.white-horsetavern.com).

Beyond the tavern is a cream-colored building set back in a field. This is the Quaker Meeting House (9). The meetinghouse was built in 1699, a time when more than half of Newport's population was Quaker. This is the oldest house of worship in the city. Additions were made in 1729 and 1807. No longer used for services, the meetinghouse is maintained by the Newport Historical Society, which can be contacted to arrange for a tour (401-846-0813; www.newporthistorical.com).

Turning your back on the tavern, look across the street to the Jailhouse Inn (1772). This is the oldest jail standing in America. Today the jailhouse is operated as a bed and breakfast.

Meeting Street is to the left of the Jailhouse Inn. Walk

one block to the end of Meeting Street, arriving at Washington Square. Known in colonial days as the Parade, this was the bustling center of 18th-century Newport, which was then a major city, as were New York, Boston, Philadelphia, and Charleston.

Look to your left. At the top of the street and the head of the square is the English Baroque, red brick Old Colony House (10), built in 1739. The architect was Richard Munday. Colony House was one of the five capitols in Rhode Island when there was one in every county. During the Revolution British troops used Colony House as a barracks; the French converted it for use as a hospital. George Washington was given a banquet here; today a full-length, life-size portrait by local artist Gilbert Stuart graces a wall. An interesting aside: several scenes from Steven Spielberg's *Amistad* were filmed inside Old Colony House and on Washington Square, which was transformed to what it might have looked like two centuries ago.

Option A: Just in back of Old Colony House, at 17 Broadway, is the Wanton-Lyman-Hazard House. Built in 1675, it is the oldest house in Newport and is opened to the public by the Newport Historical Society (401-846-0813, www.newporthistorical.org).

Look to the right down the street to the foot of the square. Note the red brick building with the colonnaded ground floor. This is the Brick Market (11). In the 1760s Peter Harrison, considered America's first architect, built this Palladian-style marketplace. Since then Brick Market has served many uses. Today it houses the Museum of Newport History (401-846-0813).

The wedge-shaped green straight ahead is Eisenhower Park (the president summered in Newport). Cross the street and take the path that cuts through the center of the park.

Stop in the middle of the park and face the courthouse, built in 1925, where Claus von Bulow had his first trial and was convicted. He was later aquitted on appeal in Providence. The story is retold in the movie *Reversal of Fortune.*

The statue at the far end of the park near the foot of the square is a monument to Oliver Hazard Perry. Perry was a Newport native and the hero of the Battle of Lake Erie during the War of 1812. Perry's famous words, "Don't give up the ship," are the motto of the U.S. Navy. Later on this tour is a monument to his brother Matthew.

Continue on the path across the center of the park, leaving opposite your point of entry. You should be at the beginning of Clarke Street, with the Jane Pickens Movie Theater on your right. Walk the full length of Clarke Street (12). The white church on the right was built in 1735 and was the Second Congregational Meeting House. The British used it as a barracks during the Revolution. It was converted to a Baptist Church in the 1830s, and much of the Greek Revival detail was added then. Today the building houses condominiums.

The church's parsonage is across the way at 14 Clarke Street. Built in 1756, the Greek Revival entryway was added later. This was the home of the Rev. Ezra Stiles, a minister, Newport cartographer, astronomer, diarist, and philosopher. When the British occupied Newport during the Revolution he and his congregation left the city. He later went on to become the president of Yale.

Next to the church is the headquarters and museum of the Newport Artillery Company. Commissioned by

King George II in 1741, this is the oldest artillery company in the country. The stone armory was built in 1835 and houses an outstanding museum of military memorablia, including a Paul Revere cannon and uniforms once worn by notables Prince Phillip, Anwar Sadat, Colin Powell, and many others. The collection is extensive and well worth a visit (401-846-8488, www.newportartillery.org).

At the end of Clarke Street you'll see the elegant 18th-century Vernon House (13) on the left. Take note of the "rusticated" facade; the wood has been carved to look like stone block. The exterior paint was mixed with sand so that it not only looks like stone but also feels like stone. When the French were in Newport during the American Revolution, Vernon House was the headquarters for General Jean-Baptiste de Rochembeau. And, yes, George Washington slept here. Today it is a private residence.

Turn left onto Mary Street. At the next corner turn right onto Spring Street and walk two blocks to Trinity Church (14).

Trinity's congregation gathered in 1698. The church, built in 1724, is another Richard Munday design, based on those by Sir Christopher Wren. The top of the 150-foot spire boasts a bishop's miter on the weathervane. Inside, note the 18th-century triple-wine-glass pulpit. Enter one of the pew boxes—at one time owned and individually decorated by parish families. Sit in pew number 81 and you'll be sitting just where George Washington sat! (401-846-0660; www.trinitynewport.org)

After visiting Trinity Church and its burial ground stand in front of the church tower for a view of Newport Harbor. This is Queen Anne's Square (15), a creation and gift of Newport summer resident Doris Duke. The square was dedicated by Queen Elizabeth during the Bicentennial in 1976. A plaque on the pavement marks the spot where she stood for the occasion.

Return to Spring Street and walk to Pelham Street. The large stone church on the left is Newport Congregational Church (16), a descendant of the Second Congregational Church seen earlier on Clarke Street. Reflecting the congregation's history, this is know as the "Church of the Patriots." The massive Romanesque structure was built in 1833. A half-century later Newport resident John LaFarge redesigned the interior with frescoes and stained-glass windows. Today it is opened by appointment (401-8499-2238, www.newportcongregationalchurch.org).

Turn left and ascend Historic Hill on Pelham Street. En route the Arnold Burial Ground (17) will be on the left. The infamous Benedict Arnold was from Newport. In fact, his great-grandfather was the first Governor of Rhode Island and a gentleman farmer who owned the surrounding acreage. The burial ground is owned and maintained by the Preservation Society of Newport County.

Stop at Touro Park, on the left. The focal point of the park is its circular tower. Known as the Old Stone Mill (18), the Viking Tower, or the Mystery Tower, its origins remain uncertain. In the early 19th century an imaginative thinker, without any evidence whatsoever, promoted the theory that in the 11th century Vikings came to this island, built the tower, and then moved on. Archaeological evidence has since proven otherwise. Most likely the tower was built in the 17th century by Benedict Arnold's great-grandfather; in his will he makes reference to his stone windmill.

Sit on one of the benches and enjoy the quiet surroundings. At the corner of Bellevue Avenue and Pelham Street, you'll see a large white house with a wraparound porch (19). This house was built in 1881 and today is the Elks' clubhouse. More noteworthy is the structure that previously stood on the site, the Atlantic House Hotel. During the Civil War, after the Battle of Bull Run (Second Manassas), Abraham Lincoln had the Naval Academy moved from Annapolis to Newport for security reasons. The Academy used Atlantic House and the midshipmen drilled in this park.

There is a stone church (20) to the right. Facing the church, in the park, is a statue of William Ellery Channing. Channing was a Newporter who became a leading abolitionist and a founder of the Unitarian movement in America. The church is his memorial, built in 1880—a century after his birth. Julia Ward Howe worshiped here, and it is said her "Battle Hymn of the Republic" was first sung in this church.

Resume your walk across the park toward Bellevue Avenue. The statue facing Bellevue Avenue is a monument to Commodore Matthew Perry, younger brother of Oliver Hazard Perry. Also a Newport native, Matthew opened Japan to the West in 1854 with his gunboat diplomacy, arriving there with his "black ships." Every July Newport commemorates Perry and celebrates everything Japanese with its Black Ships Festival.

Perry's statue faces the Newport Art Museum, which is housed in the stick-style Griswald House (21). It was an early design (1862) of Richard Morris Hunt, who later went on to design the larger and more opulent Gilded Age "cottages" farther down Bellevue Avenue.

The Newport Art Museum exhibits works by local artists as well as a series of special exhibits throughout the year (401-848-8200, www.newportartmuseum.com).

At this point you should be standing at the corner of Bellevue Avenue and Mill Street. Turn left onto Bellevue Avenue. After one block note the statue of George Washington that stands across the street from the Redwood Library (22). Another Peter Harrison design, the Redwood has the distinction of being the oldest lending library in America and the first Greek Revival building on the continent (1748). Note the Doric columns and the rusticated facade. Visit the library to see its large, old reading rooms and its impressive art collection (401-847-0292, www.redwood1747.org).

Be sure to take a close look at George Washington's statue, a bronze replica of a marble original modeled by the French sculptor Houdon. Contemporaries of Washington agreed that this was the most accurate likeness of our first president.

Continue along Bellevue Avenue. The yellow frame building at the corner of Bellevue Avenue and Church Street is the Reading Room (23), the oldest private club in America still on its original site (1854).

Cross Church Street. The red brick Georgian Revival Hotel Viking is on the left (1926). Opposite the hotel, at the corner of Kay Street, is the Old Jewish Burial Ground (24), which dates to 1658. At this point Bellevue Avenue becomes Touro Street. Descend Touro Street. The Newport Historical Society (25) will be on the right at number 82. The building contains an excellent research library and archives. The wing in back of the building is the Seventh Day Baptist Meeting House. This Richard Munday design was built in 1730. No longer used for services, the meetinghouse was moved to this site and annexed to the Historical Society building a century ago. The church exterior was originally clapboard and now has a red brick cap. The interior, however, is intact and unchanged (401-846-0813).

Just a few steps farther down Touro Street is Touro Synagogue (26). The oldest synagogue building in the Western Hemisphere, it was built between 1759 and 1763, according to plans by Peter Harrison. Harrison was not a member of the Jewish community, but he provided his services without cost. As at Brick Market, the architect was influenced by the Italian Andrea Palladio. The Touro Synagogue is a miniature reproduction of the Old Synagogue in Amsterdam, but with Palladian detail. Note that the building is at an angle to the street. This was done so that the congregation faces east, toward Jerusalem. George Washington wrote a letter to the congregation following the Revolution assuring them their religious freedom. His letter is on display inside (401-847-4794, www.tourosynagogue.org).

The walking tour ends here. To return to the Gateway Visitor Center, continue to down Touro Street to Thames Street. Walk one block farther, the length of Long Wharf Mall, to America's Cup Avenue. The Gateway will be on your right.

31 · Newport: The Bellevue Avenue Mansions

Directions: *By car:* From MA 128 take MA 24 south through Fall River and into Rhode Island. Stay on MA/RI 24 south until it ends, merging with RI 114. Take RI 114 south to Newport. Turn left onto Thames Street to America's Cup Avenue, and then left again, taking Memorial Boulevard to the corner of Bellevue Avenue. En route, driving up the hill on Memorial Boulevard, you will pass St. Mary's Church on your right. John F. Kennedy and Jacqueline Bouvier were married at St. Mary's in 1952. *By public transportation:* Direct service from Boston's South Station and from New York's Port Authority Bus Terminal is provided by Bonanza Bus Lines (1-888-751-8800, www.bonanzabus.com). From the Gateway Center in Newport, take a RIPTA bus (Yellow or Orange Line) to the corner of Memorial Boulevard and Bellevue Avenue (1-800-244-0444, www.ripta.com).

This walking tour of Bellevue Avenue includes many of Newport's fabled mansions. These were built as summer "cottages" during the Gilded Age, which began late in the 19th century and ended early in the 20th

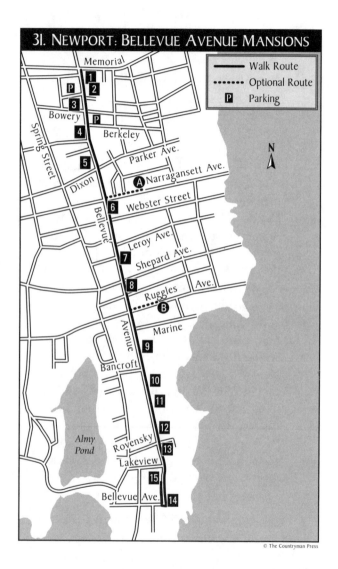

31. NEWPORT: BELLEVUE AVENUE MANSIONS

Legend:
— Walk Route
····· Optional Route
P Parking

Memorial

1
2

P

3

Bowery

P

4

Berkeley

Spring Street

Parker Ave.

5

Dixon

A Narragansett Ave.

6 Webster Street

Bellevue

Leroy Ave.

7

Shepard Ave.

8

Ruggles Ave.

B

Marine

Avenue

9

Bancroft

10

11

12

13

Almy Pond

Rovensky

Lakeview

15

Bellevue Ave. 14

N

© The Countryman Press

with income taxes and the Great Depression. But the Gilded Age social elite were not the first to flock to this, "America's first resort." Sited as it is at the southern tip of an island with the Atlantic Ocean to the south and east and the placid Narragansett Bay on the west, Newport has always enjoyed an idyllic climate. Indians made an annual migration from points inland to what they called Aquidneck, Isle of Peace, to escape the inland heat and mosquitoes. They would camp for the season, fish the surrounding waters, and plant their summer gardens.

In colonial times Newport quickly gained a reputation as a summer refuge. Many would come here to escape the Carolina and Georgia heat. But this thriving colonial port city never recovered from the Revolutionary War, and in the 19th century was but a shadow of its former self. By mid-century the city rallied and became a summer haven for literati and artists. Alfred Smith developed a dirt road and its surrounding farmland into what we now know as Bellevue Avenue, one of the most enviable addresses in America. By the end of the 19th century "America's first resort" had become its most popular and fashionable.

Begin the walk at the Travers Block (1) at the southeast corner of Bellevue Avenue and Memorial Boulevard. It was designed by Richard Morris Hunt, who is often referred to as the "dean of American architecture," in 1875. Hunt used the stick style here, just as he did in 1862 at the Griswald House, now the Newport Art Museum (see page 218). This walk will showcase some of Hunt's later, grander works.

Just steps away from the Travers Block, on Memorial Boulevard, is a statue of Christopher Columbus, which was dedicated in 1952. Never neglected, the flowerbeds around the statue's base are always planted according to the season. Memorial Boulevard was widened after World War II. It had been known as the Bath Road, the main approach to Newport Beach by car, trolley, or foot.

Walk along Bellevue Avenue. The next building on the left is the Casino (2), completed in 1880 and an outstanding example of shingle-style architecture, designed by McKim, Mead, and White. Step through the archway and take a look the grass tennis courts. Originally a social club founded by newspaper publisher James Gordon Bennett, the Casino today houses the International Tennis Hall of Fame, shops, and a restaurant.

Just two doors farther down you'll see the Audrain Building, notable for its Spanish terra-cotta trim.

Across the street note the gray picket fence on the right. The fence surrounds Kingcote (3), the first Newport mansion built as a summer cottage. It was built in 1839 for Savannah, Georgia, plantation owner George Noble Jones and, in the 1860s, passed to the King family, who made their fortune in the China trade. The architect, Richard Upjohn, is most famous for Trinity Church, on Wall Street in New York City. Both Trinity and Kingscote are Gothic Revival. Kingscote is opened to the public by the Preservation Society of Newport County (PSNC). Throughout this walk you will see many PSNC houses. The contact information for all PSNC properties is the same (401-847-1000, www.newportmansions.org).

Just one block farther along Bellevue Avenue is the Isaac Bell House (4). Another McKim, Mead, and White design, the house, built in 1883, is one of the finest examples of the shingle style. It is a PSNC property and open to visitors.

The Elms (5) is the next stop. A grand summer cottage built for coal magnate Edward Julius Berwind, the house was completed in 1901 using plans by Horrace Trumbauer. Trumbauer also designed the Philadelphia Museum of Art, Widener Library at Harvard, and the campus of Duke University. Inspired by the Chateau d'Asnieres near Paris, The Elms is an 18th-century design with every modern convenience known at the time. It was the first fully electrified house in the city. The house and the restored French gardens are opened to the public by the PSNC. A special Behind the Scenes tour offers visitors a glimpse of servant life in the Gilded Age, showing their workspaces (including the coal tunnel), living quarters, and unrivaled rooftop views of the city.

Opposite The Elms is the stone Gothic house De La Salle. Designed by Dudley Newton for William Weld in 1882, the house served as a Catholic boys' high school for half a century. The house has been divided into condominiums.

Stop at the corner of Bellevue and Narragansett Avenues. Note the statue of Newporter August Belmont (6), sculpted by John Quincy Adams Ward, the "dean of American Sculpture." Behind Belmont is the headquarters for the Preservation Society of Newport County. Founded in 1945, the society has a dozen properties open to the public. Their headquarters was built in 1887 for William Osgood, and U.S. Senator Claiborne Pell's family lived here. It was later a convent school—St. Catherine's.

Option A: Chepstow is about one block down Narragansett Avenue on the left. This Italianate villa was built in 1860, designed by George Chapin Mason. Later home to the Morris family, the house contains the family's collected furniture and artwork, including some paintings by Hudson River School artists. This is another PSNC house open to visitors. Reservations are suggested.

Resume your walk along Bellevue Avenue. Just beyond Leroy Avenue, Chateau-sur-Mer (7), or Castle by the Sea, is on the left. This property on which the building sits originally extended to the ocean. It was home to three generations of the Wetmore family. The builder, William Wetmore, made his fortune in the China trade and retired to this house year-round when construction was completed in 1852. He died ten years later, leaving the house to his son George. When George married in 1869, he and his bride lived in Britain for the next ten years and toured the Continent, while Richard Morris Hunt was given the opportunity to enlarge and redesign the house. Hunt transformed it from an Italianate villa to the French Second Empire house seen today. The chateau's Chinese Moon Gate is a few steps down Shepherd Avenue. The house is open for tours by the PSNC.

As you progress along the avenue, Vernon Court (8) will be on the left. Built in 1901 and designed by architects Carrere and Hastings (who also drew plans for the New York Public Library), this 18th-century French chateau is now the National Museum of American Illustration. Works by Rockwell, Wyeth, Parrish, and others are on display. Contact the museum before visiting, as reservations may be necessary (401-851-8949, www.americanillustration.org). The Frederick Law Olmsted Park is an adjunct of the museum.

Option B: At Ruggles Avenue turn left and walk a half block to Seaview Terrace (1929). The exterior of this house was used for many years on the TV series *Dark Shadows*. Known today as the Carey Mansion, it is used as dormitory space for Salve Regina University.

The next house on Bellevue Avenue opened to the public is Rosecliff (9). Designed after the neoclassical Grand Trianon at Versailles, it was built by Stanford White in 1902 for Mrs. Hermann (Theresa Fair) Oelrichs, whose father was a discoverer of the Comstock silver lode. Rosecliff has the largest ballroom in Newport, and parts of the films *True Lies* and *Great Gatsby* were shot here.

Just a little farther down the avenue is the Astor's Beechwood (10). Mrs. Astor could comfortably fit four hundred dancers in her New York ballroom, and so she put together a list of "the 400." Touring Beechwood can be a very entertaining experience. Guides are dressed in period costume and portray the Astors, their guests, and staff. The stuccoed Italianate villa was designed by Calvert Vaux in 1851 (401-846-3772, www.astors-beechwood.com).

Marble House (11) is next. Another Richard Morris Hunt design, William K. Vanderbilt gave this, the most costly of the Newport cottages, to his wife Alva as a birthday gift in 1892. Four years later she gave him a divorce. In time she married Oliver Hazard Perry Belmont and moved into Belcourt Castle, just down the avenue. The restored Chinese Teahouse on the Marble House's grounds overlooks the Atlantic Ocean; the entire property is opened to the public by the PSNC.

Resume your walk along the avenue. The second estate on the left after Marble House features a high granite wall and wrought-iron fence enclosing a cobblestone courtyard. This is Clarendon Court (12), former home of Sunny and Claus von Bulow. Claus was accused of trying to kill his wife with an insulin overdose. He was found guilty, but later acquitted on appeal. The story is retold in the movie *Reversal of Fortune*. Clarendon Court was designed in 1902 by Horace Trumbauer, who was inspired by an 18th-century English manorhouse. Some of the outdoor scenes for *High Society* were filmed here. The house is not open to the public.

The next estate on the left is the classical revival Miramar (13). Miramar was built in 1914 for the Widener family whose son, Harry Elkins Widener, drowned on the Titanic. Both the Harry Elkins Widener Memorial Library at Harvard and Miramar are works of Horace Trumbauer. Miramar is not open to the public.

Rough Point (14) is at the end of Bellevue Avenue on the left before the right turn in the road. Built for Frederick W. Vanderbilt in 1889, this English Gothic house was acquired by James B. Duke in 1922. Duke made his fortune in tobacco and electricity. He died in 1925, leaving the house and his fortune to his 13-year-old daughter, Doris. It became her summer home. When she died, Doris Duke left the house, its furnishings, and impressive art collection to her Newport Restoration Foundation. To tour the house it is essential that you first contact the foundation (401-849-7300, www.newportrestoration.com).

Belcourt Castle (15) is across Bellevue Avenue from Rough Point. Oliver Hazard Perry Belmont, son of August Belmont, whose statue was featured earlier, built this castle in 1892 with designs by Richard Morris Hunt.

The 60-room French hunting lodge reflects Belmont's love of horses and all things medieval. Alva Vanderbilt married Belmont after her divorce from William K. Vanderbilt, moved from Marble House into Belcourt, and redecorated the castle. The collection of medieval stained-glass windows is unrivaled in this country. Antiques and objet d'art from over 30 countries are on display. Independently owned, the house is open for tours (401-849-1566, www.belcourtcastle.com).

When returning to the starting point of this tour, you have the option of making a right on Marine Avenue at Ruggles Avenue and walking the Cliff Walk back to Memorial Boulevard.

32 • Newport: The Cliff Walk

Directions: *By car:* Take MA 128 to MA 24 south through Fall River and into Rhode Island where it will merge with RI 114. Take RI 114 south to the Gateway Visitor Center. From the Gateway follow America's Cup Avenue south, turn left onto Memorial Boulevard, right onto Bellevue Avenue, and left onto Narragansett Avenue. Park for free at the end of Narragansett Avenue. *By public transportation:* Direct service from Boston's South Station and from New York's Port Authority Bus Terminal is provided by Bonanza Bus Lines (1-888-751-8800, www.bonanzabus.com). From the Gateway Center in Newport, take the RIPTA Yellow Line to the corner of Narragansett and Ochre Point Avenues (1-800-244-0444, www.ripta.com). The Cliff Walk begins one block away.

Start your walk at the end of Narragansett Avenue (1). Cliff Walk was used as a fisherman's path in colonial times and may have served the same purpose for generations of Indians. It is a perfectly delightful walk, with the Atlantic's Rhode Island Sound on one side and the mansions and their gardens on the other. The entire Cliff Walk is 3½ miles long from the beginning to the

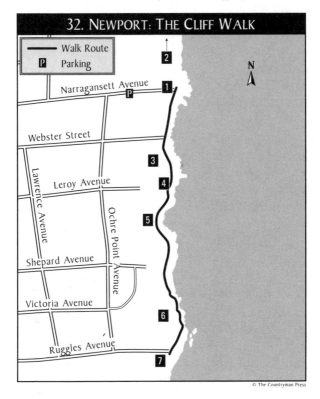

end (Memorial Boulevard to Ledge Road). This tour will not cover the entire length, but rather the most scenic and best paved portions of it.

You're standing at the top of the 40 steps. A set of wooden steps was constructed here in 1830 to provide easy access to the water below. Hurricanes have damaged a series of stairways over the years. If you have little ones with you have them count the steps (there are more than forty!). An interesting aside: during the Gilded Age the top of the steps was an evening gathering place for servants and townsfolk alike. There was music, dancing, and lots of socializing.

To your left is Newport Beach (2), otherwise known as Easton's or First Beach. The tall, square, Gothic tower on the horizon is the bell tower for St. George's School in Middletown.

Facing the ocean, turn right and walk south. After walking the length of a city block Ochre Court (3), the second largest "cottage" in Newport, is on the right. Richard Morris Hunt designed Ochre Court for Ogden Goelet in 1888. This French Gothic castle replicates King Edward VII's chateau in Paris. Ogden Goelet's son Robert made a gift of Ochre Court to the Sisters of Mercy in 1947. The house became the nucleus of Salve Regina College, which for many years was a women's college. Today SRU is a coeducational university that owns about a dozen former estates in the area.

Ochre Court is opened to the public free of charge weekdays during normal business hours. Step inside and you will be awestruck by the three-story great hall. Great central halls were a signature of Richard Morris Hunt, who featured them in other Newport mansions, such as the Breakers, Marble House, and, much earlier, the Chateau-sur-Mer. Movie buffs may find this house looks familiar. Some of the opening scenes of Arnold Schwarzenegger's *True Lies* were filmed on the snowy lawn of Ochre Court.

The next house is Cave Cliff (4), a smaller, simpler white frame house with a mansard roof, built in 1877.

Vinland (5) is the sandstone house you see next. It was designed by Peabody and Stearns in Queen Anne Revival style for the tobacco heiress Catherine Lorillard Wolfe in 1882. This later became the home of Florence

ROBERT J. REGALBUTO

The Cliff Walk

Vanderbilt Twombley, whose daughter, Florence Burden, donated this house to SRU. For many years this was the school's library. The shoebox of a building next door is SRU's O'Hare Academic Center.

Walk a few steps farther to see the grandest of the Newport mansions: The Breakers (6). This is a Vanderbilt House. Commodore Cornelius Vanderbilt (1794–1877) established his family's fortune in steamships and railroads. It was one of his grandsons—Cornelius Vanderbilt II—who purchased this property from Pierre Lorillard in 1885. The first house on the site, a wooden Peabody and Stearns Queen Anne design, burned in 1892. The present house was built between 1893 and 1895. Richard Morris Hunt was the architect. His inspiration was the Italian palazzi of Genoa and Turin. Cornelius II and his wife, Alice, had seven children. The youngest, Gladys, married the Hungarian Count Szechenyi. When her mother died the Countess inherited the Breakers. She was very generous to the Preservation Society when it was founded in 1945, leasing the

Breakers to the Society for $1.00 a year while still paying taxes on the property and making repairs to the house. The Society opened the house to the public and charged admission. The money raised helped save Hunter House, a colonial house in Newport's Point neighborhood. It also provided the vital startup funds for the Society. The countess died in 1965, and in 1972 the PSNC purchased the Breakers from her heirs for a nominal sum.

The Breakers is the largest of the Newport summer "cottages," but was designed to be lived in just six to eight weeks of the year. The area of the house is over 138,000 square feet. There are 70 rooms, the largest being the great central hall, a cube measuring 50 feet on all sides. Tours are given by the PSNC (401-847-1000, www.newportmansions.org).

The walking tour ends just beyond the Breakers at the foot of Ruggles Avenue (7). The house just across Ruggles Avenue is Anglesea (1880), a private residence. In the distance you may see the green roof and red columns of the Chinese Teahouse, on the Marble House property. The houses along the Cliff Walk that are open to visitors may be accessed from Bellevue Avenue but not from the Cliff Walk. If you wish to continue your walk here be warned that, despite the repairs made by the Army Corps of Engineers in the wake of hurricane devastation, it is not well paved from this point south. Marine Avenue (the next street south, a dirt road) is the last chance to exit Cliff Walk before its ends at Ledge Road.

If you are ending your walk here, visit the Breakers if you like by walking around the corner to the front gate. RIPTA's Yellow Line has frequent service from the Breakers to the Gateway Visitors Center.

33 · Bristol

Directions: *By car:* From MA 128 take MA 24 south, which becomes RI 24. In Portsmouth, Rhode Island, take exit 2. Then take RI 114 north over the Mount Hope Bridge. Continue on RI 114 north (Hope Street) to downtown Bristol. *By public transportation:* Bonanza Bus Lines (1-888-751-8800, www.bonanzabus. com), MBTA Commuter Rail (1-800-392-6100, www.mbta.com), and AMTRAK (1-800-USA-RAIL, www.amtrak.com) all offer service to Providence. From Kennedy Plaza in Providence take RIPTA bus #60 (the Newport bus) from the Q stop to the corner of Hope and State Streets in Bristol (401-781-9400, 1-800-244-0444, www.ripta.com).

Settlers from Plymouth Colony established Bristol in 1681, naming it after their home in England. Originally a part of Massachusetts Bay Colony, Bristol was transferred to Rhode Island and Providence Plantations in 1746. A thriving port in colonial times, during the American Revolution Bristol suffered under British attacks in 1775 and again in 1778. The commercial port never recovered. Narragansett Bay is now home to many recreational yachts, some of which you may see under sail during your walking tour.

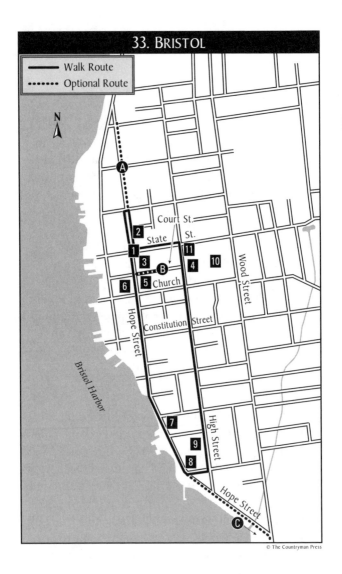

33. BRISTOL

- ——— Walk Route
- ·········· Optional Route

N

Ⓐ

Court St.

2

State St.

1

3

Ⓑ

11

4

10

5

6

Church

Hope Street

Constitution Street

Wood Street

Bristol Harbor

7

High Street

9

8

Hope Street

Ⓒ

© The Countryman Press

Begin at the intersection of historic Bristol's two main thoroughfares: Hope and State Streets (1). Walk north on Hope Street just a half block to Linden Place (2). The Federal-style mansion was designed by Russell Warren, a Bristol native. Built in 1810 for General George DeWolf, the house was later lived in by the Colts, who made their fortune manufacturing firearms, and later the Barrymores, a family of notable actors including Ethel, Lionel, and John Drew. A distinctive octagonal, Gothic Revival conservatory is a part of the house. The gardens feature an 18th-century summer house and over two dozen statues depicting animals, birds, and classical figures. Both house and gardens are open to visitors (401-253-0390; www.lindenplace.org).

Just steps away, on Wardell Street, is Linden Place's ballroom (1905) which now houses the Bristol Art Museum. An early 19th-century DeWolf coach is on permanent display; other exhibits change seasonally.

After Linden Place continue north on Hope Street. The large, white marble, classical building on your right is the Colt Memorial School. The school was donated to the town by Samuel Pomeroy Colt in 1906.

Option A: Continue north on Hope as far as Washington Street to see a number of well-preserved 18th- and 19th-century residences. Numbers 617 and 647 are Russell Warren, Greek Revival designs, both built in 1838. Number 631 is an 1855 Italianate house. Three late-18th-century houses are clustered closer to Washington Street: numbers 649, 693, and 736. The large, rambling classical revival building on your right is the Guiteras School.

Reverse direction and walk south on Hope Street. Note the Rogers Free Library on the right. The present library replaces an earlier building destroyed by fire in the 1950s. The brownstone portico salvaged from the old library belies the modern building within.

The post office next door is essentially a cinder-block cube, its facade fitted with windows, moulding, urns and the like salvaged from a house that once stood on this site.

Cross State Street and continue to walk on Hope Street. There will be a Tudor-style building (3), built in 1898, on the left. The red brick Italianate building next door, set back from the street a few feet, was built in 1857 and once served as the federal presence in town, housing the customhouse and the post office.

The next street on the left is Court Street. At the head of this street you can see the courthouse (4). Later the tour will pass the building's front door for a closer view.

Option B: The Bristol Historical and Preservation Society's Museum is at 48 Court Street in the 1828 building that once housed the Bristol County Jail (401-253-7223).

The Burnside Memorial Building (5) at the corner of Court and Hope Streets was named to honor one of Bristol's most famous residents: Civil War General Ambrose Burnside. "Sideburns" got their name from the general, who sported whiskers at the side of his face in a distinctive style. His memorial building, constructed in 1883, houses town offices.

The statue *Soldiers and Sailors* was dedicated in 1914 and modeled by Henri Schonhardt. The Bristol War Veteran Honor Roll Garden is just behind the statue. The brownstone building on the left is the parish house for St. Michael's Episcopal Church, built in 1877. The Cherry Memorial Bell Tower was completed in 1962.

On the opposite side of Hope Street is St. Michael's Church (6), founded in 1718 as a mission of the Church of England. This, the third church building to serve the parish, was built in 1860. The massive stone bell tower was added in 1891. Step inside and look at the exceptional collection of stained-glass windows. The window behind the high altar depicts St. Michael the Archangel slaying a dragon. This is a Tiffany reproduction of a Raphael painting. The garden, or close, alongside the church and the central cross are memorials dedicated in 1920 to the Rev. George Lyman Locke, rector from 1867 to 1919.

Resume your walk up Hope Street, which will abut the harbor on your right. On your left, at Burnside Street, is the Herreshoff Marine Museum (7). The world's finest yachts were manufactured here by the Herreshoff family from 1863 to 1945. A series of eight yachts, all successful America's Cup defenders from 1893 to 1934, were built here. The museum includes the America's Cup Hall of Fame, the Hall of Boats, and a room filled with exceptional boat models. In all, the collection of yachts on display is considered the finest in America (401-253-5000, www.herreshoff.org).

Walk another block up Hope Street. On the left, at the corner of Walley Street, you will see a stone Gothic Revival house (8) designed by James Renwick in the 1870s. Renwick is well known for designing other Gothic Revival buildings, including the Smithsonian Castle in Washington, D.C., and St. Patrick's Cathedral in New York City.

Option C: Walk about a mile farther along the waterfront to Blithewold, an early 19th-century mansion and gardens open to visitors. Built in the style of a

17th-century English manor house, the 45-room mansion sits on the banks of the bay and is surrounded by 33 acres of fields, gardens, and two hundred varieties of trees and shrubs. A highlight of the year is when the estate's 50,000 daffodils bloom in spring. Marjorie Van Wickle Lyon, daughter of the builder, lived here until her death in 1976 at the age of 93. In keeping with her wishes, Blithewold is open to visitors (401-253-2707, www.blithewold.org).

You are about to leave Hope Street and return downtown. Go up Walley Street and then turn left onto High Street. On the left at 41 High Street is an octagonal house (9), built in 1846. Octagonal houses are curiosities left over from the mid-1800s, the invention of Orson S. Fowler. Fowler promoted the notion that eight-sided houses were a better use of space, were economical to build, and had better ventilation and more sunlight than conventional houses. A few thousand of them were built; a few hundred remain standing today.

Continue along High Street. After crossing Church Street the town common will be on your right. Take a closer look at the Bristol County Court House (10), built in 1817. This initially served as one of Rhode Island's five statehouses; there was one in each county. Opened to the public, the second floor of this Federal-style building is being restored to its original appearance (401-253-0015).

Three churches surround the town common. Next door to the courthouse stands Bristol's oldest church building, the First Baptist Church (11), constructed in 1814. The Gothic Revival St. Mary's Roman Catholic Church at the far side of the common was built in 1911 for the French community. Our Lady of Mount Carmel

Church, the red brick church on your left, was built by Bristol's Italians in 1918.

Walk past the First Baptist Church to the corner of State Street. From High Street turn left onto State Street, returning to the corner of Hope and State Streets where this tour began. This block has three Russell Warren houses, at numbers 86, 89, 92. Number 86 was the architect's own home. At the conclusion of the walking tour you may wish to walk down State Street one more block to the waterfront, where there are parks, docks, shops, and restaurants.

IV. Connecticut

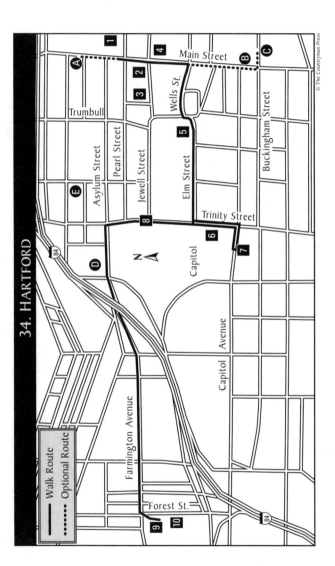

34. HARTFORD

34 • Hartford

Directions: *By car:* Take I-90, the Massachusetts Turnpike, west to I-84, exit 9, then take I-84 west to exit 52 and follow the signs to the Old State House. *By public transportation:* Three bus companies offer service to Hartford: Bonanza Bus Line (1-888-751-8800, www.bonanzabus.com), Peter Pan Bus Lines (1-800-343-9999, www.peterpanbus.com), and Greyhound Lines (1-800-231-2222, www.greyhound.com). AMTRAK also has service to Hartford (1-800-USA-RAIL, www.amtrak.com).

Dutch traders from New Amsterdam were the first Europeans to arrive in this area in 1633. Two years later 60 English colonists settled here permanently. Led by Thomas Hooker and the Rev. Samuel Stone, they were members of the First Church of Christ in Cambridge (then Newtowne), Massachusetts. Today's Center Church houses the descendant congregation of those settlers. They named the town after Reverend Stone's birthplace: Hertford, in Herfordshire, England. The group wrote the Fundamental Orders of Connecticut as their governing document. In 1687, when Governor Andros tried to rescind the document, it was hidden in an old oak tree, which became known as the Charter

Oak. The Fundamental Orders of Connecticut was later a model for the U.S. Constitution, and so Connecticut is often dubbed the Constitution State.

Hartford and New Haven were both state capitals until 1875, when Hartford became the sole capital. The city is also an insurance capital. In 1794 the first Hartford fire insurance policy was sold. Today the city is home base to nearly 50 insurance companies.

The Old State House (1), designed by Bostonian Charles Bulfinch in 1796, stands on the site of a previous capitol, which burned in 1783. Fully restored in 1996, the Old State House is opened to visitors. There are guided tours. Highlights include a Gilbert Stuart portrait of George Washington and Joseph Steward's old Museum of Curiosities. The first *Amistad* trial took place here, and historic reenactments are presented (860-522-6766, www.ctosh.org).

Option A: Christ Church Cathedral (Episcopal) is close to the Old State House at the corner of Main and Church Streets. Founded in 1762, the present church was designed in 1827 by New Haven's Ithiel Towne and is one of the first Gothic Revival churches on this side of the Atlantic. Many of its features were inspired by those seen at British churches, such as Westminster Abbey and York Minster. The brown exterior stone was quarried in Portland, Connecticut, and transported to Hartford on the Connecticut River. The cathedral's wall are 3 feet thick, and the 150-foot-high bell tower houses a chime of 12 bells (860-527-7237, www.cccathedral.org).

With your back to the Old State House turn left and walk along Main Street. Note the white, three-tiered spire of South Congregational (or Center) Church (2) on the right at the corner of Gold Street. Built in 1807, the model for this building was the Church of St. Martin-in-the-Fields in London. It has five Tiffany stained-glass windows. The church is closely associated with Hartford's founders. Connecticut ratified the U.S. Constitution in the churchyard in 1788.

Enter the Ancient Burying Ground (3) through the gate just a few steps from the church. This was Hartford's only burial ground from 1640 to 1800, and it is estimated that 6,000 people are buried here. An excellent descriptive brochure is available (860-561-2585).

Turn right as you leave the cemetery gate and continue on Main Street. The Gothic Revival building across the street on the left is the Wadsworth Atheneum (4), which has the distinction of being America's oldest public art museum. It was founded in 1841 by Daniel Wadsworth, who donated his family homestead as the site for the museum, and others. A Gothic Revival gallery was completed in 1844. In 1910 two wings were added: the Renaissance Revival Morgan Memorial, which contains J. P. Morgan's art collection, and the Tudor-style Colt Memorial, given in memory of firearms manufacturer Samuel Colt. Two modern wings, the Avery Memorial (1932) and the James Lippincott Goodwin Building (1965), complete the complex. Unfortunately the original Gothic Revival gallery has been gutted, its interior stripped of period detail in favor of a more utilitarian, modern space. The atheneum's collection includes almost fifty thousand objects and is comprehensive: ancient art, European works spanning the 16th through 20th centuries, American painting, sculpture and decorative arts from colonial times to the present, and two galleries of African American art, as well as the largest collection of Hudson River

School paintings anywhere (860-278-2670, www.wadsworthatheneum.org).

Option B: The Butler-McCook Homestead, at 396 Main Street, near Charter Oak Avenue, is a short walk from the atheneum. Built in 1782, it was given to the Antiquarian and Landmarks Society in 1971 by its last occupant, Frances McCook. The house has a large exhibit of 18th- and 19th-century American decorative arts and memorabilia (860-247-8996). The Homestead Gardens overlook the Amos Bull House (1788).

Option C: The Charter Oak Cultural Center, at 21 Charter Oak Avenue, was built in 1876 and was Connecticut's first synagogue. On the National Register of Historic Places, its interior retains original stained-glass windows and stenciling. The synagogue was restored in the 1980s and is now used as a cultural center (860-249-1207).

Walk to the corner of Main and Wells Streets. Walk along Wells Street to Pulaski Circle and then up Elm Street toward the state capitol. The 37-acre Bushnell Park is on the right. Developed in 1854, it was the first public park in America. The Pump House Gallery (5) is near the circle. This charming, English Tudor–style house was built by the Army Corps of Engineers in 1947 to house a pumping station for flood control. Today it houses an art gallery and restaurant.

Visit the State Capitol (6), built in 1878 and designed by Richard Upjohn. The Victorian High Gothic building has an exterior of marble and granite embellished with bas reliefs, statues, and medallions—all recounting the history of Connecticut and its heroes. The gilded dome is surrounded by 12 allegorical figures representing agriculture, commerce, education, science,

MARK TWAIN MEMORIAL

The Mark Twain House

music, and force. Atop the dome stands a bronze statue of a winged woman. Entitled the *Genius of Connecticut,* the statue was cast in Munich, Germany. The inside of the capital is also highly decorated in the Victorian fashion with stenciling, stained glass, statuary, and patterned marble floors. Tours are graciously provided by the League of Women Voters of Connecticut (860-240-0222).

Walk down the hill to Capitol Avenue. En route note the outstanding variety of mature trees: oak, maple, sycamore, and magnolia, to name a few. Cross Capitol Avenue to the State Library and Supreme Court building. The Connecticut Museum of History (7) is inside; the museum's nucleus is Memorial Hall. A beaux-arts room, it was built in 1910 and has recently been restored. The museum's collection is eclectic and offers something for almost any student of Connecticut history: governors' portraits, historic documents (including the Royal Charter of 1662), the Colt firearms collection, the Mitchelson coin collection, and the Connecticut collection, with artifacts reflecting the state's political, military, and industrial histories (860-757-6535, www. cslib.org).

After leaving the museum, walk straight down Trinity Street to the Soldiers' and Sailors' Memorial Arch (8). A Civil War monument, the arch is dedicated to the four thousand Hartford citizens who fought in the war and the four hundred who died in service. Completed in 1886, the Connecticut brownstone Gothic arch was designed by George Keller. Both Keller and his wife are buried in the east tower. Surrounding the turrets are 8-foot statues placed in niches, each representing servicemen called from various professions: a farmer, a student, a freed slave, a stonemason, a carpenter, and a blacksmith. Above the arch a terra-cotta frieze surrounds the entire monument, its bas reliefs depicting scenes from the Civil War. The turrets are topped with bronze statues of the archangels Raphael and Gabriel. The arch was restored in 1987. Climb to the top for a bird's-eye view of the capitol and the city.

The carousel to the right as you approach the arch was made in 1914, stood in Canton, Ohio, for 60 years, and was moved to Hartford and restored in 1974. Note the Werlitzer Band Organ and the 48 hand-carved horses and two chariots.

The next stop is Mark Twain's House, about one mile from Bushnell Park; there is little of note between here and there. You have the option of walking to Mark Twain's House or driving. Walk or drive along Trinity Street to Asylum Street. Turn left onto Asylum Street. At the fork in the road bear left onto Farmington Avenue. Mark Twain's House will be on the left.

En route to the house is St. Joseph's Roman Catholic

Cathedral (on the right on Farmington Avenue). A modern design, it was built in 1962 to replace a cathedral that was destroyed by fire in 1956. That cathedral was a very large Gothic Revival church built in 1892.

Option D: Union Station, at Asylum Street and Union Place, is 100 years old and functions as Hartford's transportation center. Restored, the station is the arrival and departure point for trains and busses, and houses a number of eateries and shops (860-247-5329).

Option E: St. Patrick and St. Anthony Church, at Church and Ann Streets, is Connecticut's oldest Roman Catholic parish. A Portland, Connecticut, brownstone building, its interior was restored in 1988.

The Mark Twain House (9) is very popular. It was built in 1874 for Twain; he spent some of the happiest and most productive years of his life here. *The Adventures of Tom Sawyer* and *The Adventures of Huckleberry Finn* were published during his Hartford years. The rambling stick-style mansion's interior has the only Louis Comfort Tiffany–designed rooms surviving today. Guided tours of the house last an hour (860-247-0998, ext. 26, www.marktwainhouse.org).

Just steps away from Twain's House is Harriet Beecher Stowe's house (10), built in 1871. Her writings, including *Uncle Tom's Cabin*, advanced the abolitionists' cause. Start your visit at the Stowe Center, which is located in the old carriage house. Guided tours are available (860-522-9258, www.hartnet.org/stowe).

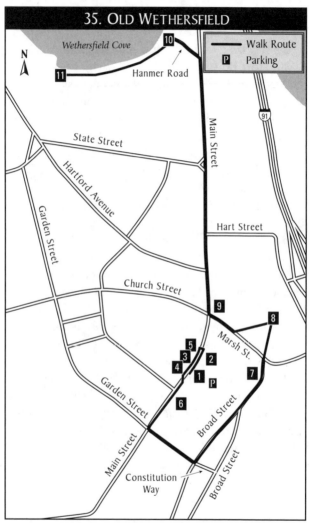

35. OLD WETHERSFIELD

Wethersfield Cove

Hanmer Road

N

Wethersfield Cove

— Walk Route

P Parking

State Street

Hartford Avenue

Garden Street

Main Street

91

Hart Street

Church Street

9

8

Marsh St.

5
3
4
2
1
P

7

6

Garden Street

Broad Street

Main Street

Constitution Way

Broad Street

© The Countryman Press

35 · Old Wethersfield

Directions: *By car:* Take I-90, the Massachusetts Turnpike, west to exit 9, I-84 west. Take
exit 52 to I-91 south. Take exit 26 and follow
the signs to Wethersfield. *By public transportation:* Three bus companies offer service to
Hartford: Bonanza Bus Line (1-888-751-
8800, www.bonanzabus.com), Peter Pan Bus
Lines (1-800-343-9999, www.peterpanbus.
com), and Greyhound Lines (1-800-231-
2222, www.greyhound.com). AMTRAK also
has service to Hartford (1-800-USA-RAIL,
www.amtrak.com). From Union Station in
Hartford, walk or take any CTTransit bus to
Center Church, at Main and Gold Streets.
Then take CTTransit bus number U2 to Old
Wethersfield (860-525-9181, www.cttransit.
com).

Wethersfield, founded in 1634, is the oldest permanent English settlement in the Nutmeg State.
Named for Wethersfield, England, the colonial town
prospered as a Connecticut River port.

A good introduction to Old Wethersfield is the
Wethersfield Museum at the Keeney Cultural Center,
200 Main Street (1). Built as a school in 1893, the
building is now owned and operated by the Wethers-

field Historical Society (860-529-7656, www.weth-hist.org).

From the museum turn right onto Main Street to the Hurlbut-Dunham House (2) at number 212. The house is unique in that it was built in the 18th century and its exterior was modified in the 1860s to the then-fashionable Italianate style. The interior was decorated in the 20th century in Colonial Revival style. Tours of the house start at the Wethersfield Museum.

Cross Main Street to the Joseph Webb House (3) at number 211. It is one of a group of three historic house museums which, combined, are known as the Webb-Deane-Stevens Museum (860-529-0612, www.webb-deane-stevens.org). The Webb House was built in 1752. In 1781 George Washington and Comte de Rochembeau met in this house to plan the Battle of Yorktown. And, yes, George Washington slept here. His bedroom has the same flocked wallpaper he saw during his stay. The Webb barn is also open.

The Silas Deane House (4), built in 1766, is the second house in the group. It is notable for its hand-carved mahogany staircase and its eight elegantly furnished rooms.

The third house is the Isaac Stevens House (5), a dwelling built in 1788 for a middle-class family. There is a period garden in back of the house that includes an herb garden.

With your back to the Stevens House, turn right on Main Street. The Old Academy (6), constructed in 1894, will be across the street at number 150. This building once served as town hall, town library, and as a girls' academy. The red brick building is now the headquarters and library for the Wetherfield Historical Society

(860-529-7656, www.wethhist.org).

Walk farther along Main Street and turn left onto Garden Street. When you reach the Broad Street Green turn left again. The Buttolph-Williams House (7) will be on the left at number 249. The house was built for a tanner in 1692. Furnished to the period, the kitchen is the focal point of this house (860-529-0460).

Walk to the Ancient Burial Ground (8), which dates to 1648, at the end of Broad Street. Turn left onto Marsh Street to the corner of Main Street. The First Church of Christ (9) will be on the right. The congregation gathered in 1635. This, the third meetinghouse to stand on this site, was built in 1764. It is the oldest brick church in Connecticut (860-529-1575, www.firstchurch.org).

Turn right onto Main Street and turn left onto Hanmer Road to the Cove Warehouse (10). Dating to the 1600s, this is the only one of seven warehouses to survive a devastating flood in 1692. Open to the public by the Wethersfield Historical Society, the warehouse has exhibits on local maritime history.

Finish the tour at Cove Park (11) overlooking the Connecticut River and enjoy the view.

36 · New Haven and Yale University

Directions: *By car:* Take I-90, the Massachusetts Turnpike, west to exit 9 and I-84 west. Take I-84 exit 52 to I-91 south. In New Haven take exit 3 and follow the signs to Yale. *By public transportation:* AMTRAK (1-800-USA-RAIL; www.amtrak.com) and two bus companies offer service to New Haven: Peter Pan Bus Lines (1-800-343-9999, www.peterpanbus.com) and Greyhound Lines (1-800-231-2222, www.greyhound.com).

New Haven was founded in 1638 by Puritans and was originally known as Quinnipiac—the same name given to the town's river. In 1640 the colonists renamed the town after Newhaven, in Sussex, England. This grew to New Haven Colony, which, in 1664, joined the Connecticut Colony, then based in Hartford. From 1701 to 1875 both New Haven and Hartford were co-capitals of the Nutmeg State.

New Haven is a city of inventors. Residents included Charles Goodyear (vulcanized rubber), Eli Whitney (cotton gin), and Samuel Colt (revolvers). In the 19th century the city was a center for the abolitionist movement. Yale University, founded in 1701, was named for Elihu Yale, a wealthy London merchant who gave the

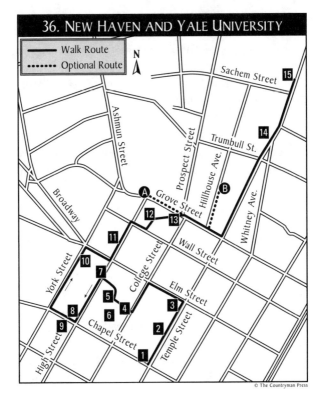

36. NEW HAVEN AND YALE UNIVERSITY

newly founded school a library of four hundred books, a donation of more than five hundred pounds, and a portrait of King George I.

The Puritans planned New Haven as a large square divided into nine smaller squares. Central to these squares was the 16-acre green, where the tour starts. It was first used by the entire community as a burial ground, pasture, and parade ground; three churches were built on the perimeter of the green early in the 19th century, each representing a distinct Christian tradition and architectural style.

Begin at Trinity Church (1), at the corner of Chapel and Temple Streets. This Anglican-Episcopal parish was founded in 1852 and for more than 50 years worshiped in a wooden church that stood at Church and Chapel Streets. The present church, an early attempt at Gothic Revival, was built in 1813. The architect was Ithiel Town. Visit the inside and see the exceptionally fine collection of stained-glass windows, some of which were made by Tiffany (203-624-3101, www.trinitynewhaven. org).

Walk along Temple Street to Center Church (2). This congregation is a descendant of the Puritans who founded New Haven. The building (1812–15) is the fourth built on this site. Interestingly, part of the church covers the colonial burial ground. The crypt and burial ground are open to visitors for tours, but contact the church in advance. Above the crypt be sure to see the Georgian-style church designed by Asher Benjamin. Ithiel Town, Trinity's architect, was the builder of Center Church. Inspired by the works of Sir Christopher Wren, this is considered the finest of the three churches on the green. Note the Tiffany stained-glass window over the pulpit. More than two thousand pieces of glass unite to form a brilliant depiction of the first religious service held in New Haven by the Puritans in 1683 (203-787-0121).

The third church is the United Church-on-the-Green (3). This congregation separated from the established church of New Haven in 1742, during the religious movement known as the Great Awakening. It is now a congregation of the United Church of Christ. The Federal-style church was built in 1812–15 and designed by

Ebenezer Johnson. While the exterior has remained unaltered, the interior saw major changes in 1849 and again in 1966. The abolitionist Henry Ward Beecher preached here (203-787-4195, www.newlights.org).

From the United Church make a left at the corner to Elm Street, and another left onto College Street. Enter Yale University (203-432-2300, www.yale.edu/visitor/) through the Phelps Gate (4) on your right. This and the surrounding Victorian High Gothic building are the core of the old campus. Directly in front of you is a statue of Theodore Dwight Woosley, a 19th-century university president. Be sure to rub his well-worn toe for good luck, as students have done for generations. The statue stands in front of Dwight Hall (5). Built in 1846 to designs by Henry Austin, this was Yale's first Gothic Revival building. Once the Old Library, Dwight now houses, among other things, a chapel.

Connecticut Hall (6) is on the left. This 1753 red-brick Georgian building is the oldest structure in New Haven. A statue of alumnus Nathan Hale (class of 1773), who lived in Connecticut Hall, stands nearby.

Walk to the right of Dwight Hall to High Street, where there are two more monuments to university presidents: Abraham Pierson, the first president (1701–1707), and a bench dedicated to A. Bartlett Giamatti, president from 1978 to 1986 and later the Major League Baseball commissioner.

The Gothic Revival Harkness Tower (7) is on High Street. Built in 1921 "for God, for Country, and for Yale," the Memorial Room at the base of the tower is embellished with wood paneling chiseled with figures representing Yale's history, notables, and students. The 216-foot-tall tower houses a carillon of 54 English bells.

Walk along High Street to Chapel Street, and then turn right. You are now flanked by two outstanding art museums: Yale University Art Gallery (8) on the right and the Yale Center for British Art (9) on the left.

The Art Gallery has the distinction of being the oldest college art museum in the Western Hemisphere. It began in 1832 with a major donation of works by John Trumbull. Trumbull was a Connecticut native, an artist, and a patriot. As the collection grew to include other works, so did the museum's facilities. In 1928 the Italian Gothic art gallery was built; the adjacent modern wing was designed by Louis I. Kahn and added in 1953. The museum's collection is vast and varied: ancient, African, Asian, pre-Columbian, and European (early Italian to contemporary) art, and a truly noteworthy collection of works by American artists: Trumbull, Copley, Homer, Eakins, Hopper, and others. American decorative arts complete the collection. Special exhibits are mounted throughout the year (203-432-0600, www.yale.edu/artgallery/).

The Yale Center for British Art has the finest collection of British art and rare books outside of Britain. The collection was a gift of Paul Mellon (class of 1929) and the award-winning building housing it, constructed in 1977, is another Louis I. Kahn work (203-432-2800, www.yale.edu/ycba/).

Walk along Chapel Street and turn right onto York Street. On York Street the Wexham Tower (10) will be on your right. Elihu Yale is buried in Wexham, England, and the tower replicates the one at that town's St. Giles Church.

Turn right onto Elm Street and then left to Sterling Memorial Library (11). The library was named in honor

YALE UNIVERSITY

Yale University

of John William Sterling, a Yale alumnus (class of 1864) and the university's major benefactor. Best described as "modern Gothic" the library, designed by James Gamble Rogers, was completed in 1930. The interior features a mural, stained-glass windows, sculpture, and wrought iron celebrating the history of Yale and the history of writing and books. Include the Exhibition Corridor and Memorabilia Room in your visit (203-432-4771, www. library.yale.edu).

Just outside the door of the library on your right is the granite fountain named the *Women's Table*. Designed in 1993 by Yale alumna Maya Lin, the sculpture is dedicated to all women who have studied at Yale. The art school admitted the university's first female students in 1873; the undergraduate school became coeducational in 1969. Lin's best known work is the Vietnam Memorial in Washington, D.C.

Stand with your back to Sterling Memorial Library. Walk through Cross Campus and turn left after Berkeley Hall. The Beinecke Rare Book and Manuscript Library (12) will be on your left. Designed by Gordon Burnshaft in 1963, the library must be seen from the inside to appreciate its most unique feature: exterior walls made of hundreds of squares of translucent Vermont marble. A Gutenberg Bible and other books and manuscripts are on permanent display (203-432-2977, www. library.yale.edu/beinecke).

The three marble sculptures in front of Beinecke Library are the work of Japanese American artist Isamu Noguchi. The University Commons (a dining hall) is on the left, its facade a World War I memorial. Woosley Hall (a theater) is on the right. Walk through the rotunda of Memorial Hall (13). Its walls are inscribed with the names of Yale alumni who served in U.S. wars, starting with the American Revolution. The Civil War memorial was designed by Henry Bacon, who also designed Washington's Lincoln Memorial. Exit Memorial Hall at the corner of College and Grove Streets.

Option A: The Grove Street Cemetery (1796) is just across the street. It includes the graves of Eli Whitney, Noah Webster, Charles Goodyear, and many Yale presidents. Access the cemetery through the Egyptian Revival gate (Henry Austin, 1845) at Grove and High Streets.

Walk along Grove Street toward Hillhouse Avenue.

Option B: The Yale Collection of Musical Instruments is located at 15 Hillhouse Avenue. The permanent exhibit includes American and European instruments from the 16th through 20th centuries (203-432-0822). Just a few steps away is St. Mary's Roman Catholic Church. The Gothic Revival church was built in 1876. The Knights of Columbus, an international fraternity, was founded at St. Mary's in 1881, and now maintains its headquarters and museum in New Haven.

As you walk on Grove Street turn left onto Temple Street, which will merge with Whitney Avenue. The New Haven Colony Historical Society (14) museum and library is at 14 Whitney Avenue. Several galleries review and document New Haven's history, highlighting locals Eli Whitney and Charles Goodyear. Also on display are artifacts from the slave ship *Amistad* (203-562-4183).

Walk on Whitney Avenue to the corner of Sachem Street. The Yale Peabody Museum of Natural History (15) is on the left. The museum's collection was started in the 18th century, grew in the 19th, and moved to this, its permanent home, in the 20th. The focal point of this 1925 building is the two-story Great Hall. The skeletal remains of prehistoric dinosaurs are here; the tallest stands 67 feet high. Also in the Great Hall: a Pulitzer Prize–winning 110-foot-long mural by Rudolph F. Zallinger. Depicting the Age of the Reptiles, this was a 3½-year project completed in 1947. The other per-

manent exhibits include wildlife dioramas, birds, minerals, and mammals (203-432-5050, www.peabody.
yale.edu).

V. New Hampshire

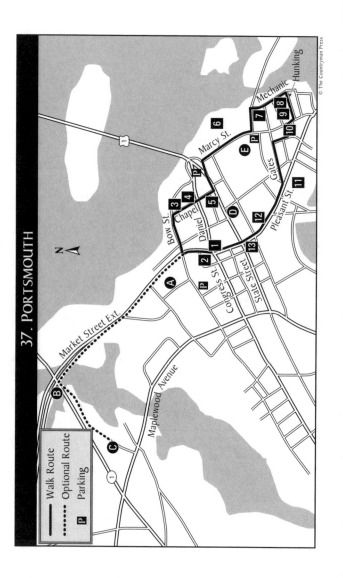

37. PORTSMOUTH

N

Market Street Ext.

Maplewood Avenue

Bow St.

Chapel

Daniel

Congress St.

State Street

Pleasant St.

Marcy St.

Mechanic

Hunking

Gates

Walk Route

Optional Route

P Parking

© The Countryman Press

37 · Portsmouth

Directions: *By car:* Take I-95 north to exit 7. Turn right and follow Market Street to Market Square. *By public transportation:* Two bus companies offer service to Portsmouth: C&J Trailways (1-800-258-7111, www.cjtrailways.com) and Vermont Transit (1-800-642-3133, www.vermonttransit.com).

Portsmouth has the distinction of being New Hampshire's oldest settlement and its only seaport. Founded as a fishing center along the shore of the Piscataqua River in 1623, the town was first named for the river and later, more picturesquely, Strawbery Banke. In 1653 the town was incorporated and named for Portsmouth, England. With its thriving harbor, Portsmouth was an English provincial capital in colonial times and later became New Hampshire's first state capital. An important part of the local economy has been the Naval Shipyard, which opened in 1790.

Market Square (1) is the starting point for this walk through Portsmouth. In colonial days the square was the city's bustling center, a parade ground surrounded by the capitol, market stalls, and the old meetinghouse (1713). The red brick Italianate North Church (1854) stands on the site of the old meetinghouse.

Opposite the front door of the church is the

Athenaeum (2) at 9 Market Square. This Federal-style building dates to 1803. Step inside and see the Athenaeum's collection of portraits and objects relating to the city's history (603-431-2538).

As you face the Athenaeum, Market Street will be on the right. Walk along Market Street to Bow Street.

Option A: Continue down Market Street past the 19th-century warehouses known as Merchants Row. The Moffatt-Ladd House is at 154 Market Street. Built in 1763, the house was occupied by the same family for generations. William Whipple, a signer of the Declaration of Independence, lived here. The house is maintained by the Colonial Dames of America, who open its doors to visitors (603-436-8221).

Option B: Continue down Market Street Extension to Albacore Park on the shores of the Piscataqua River. Here you may visit the submarine U.S.S. *Albacore*, which was built here in Portsmouth using the most up-to-date mid-20th-century technology. The park also has a memorial garden honoring those who have lost their lives in submarines (603-436-3680).

Option C: The Richard Jackson House is near the park at 76 Northwest Street. Dating to 1664, this is the oldest surviving wood-frame house in New Hampshire. The Jackson family lived here until the house was acquired in 1923 by the Society for the Preservation of New England Antiquities, who now open the house to visitors (603-436-3205, www.spnea.org).

From Market Street turn onto Bow Street. Walk past the early 19th-century red brick warehouses and pause to enjoy the view of the Piscataqua River on your left. Turn right onto Chapel Street. St. John's Episcopal Church (3) will be on the left. This is the second church to serve the parish. The original Queen Anne's Chapel (1732) burned in Portsmouth's Great Christmas Eve Fire in 1806. The present church was built the following year to plans by the noted Federal-period architect Alexander Parris. A number of items survive from the first church, among them a French steeple bell (recast at Paul Revere's foundry following the fire), the chair in which George Washington sat at services, sterling silver communion vessels presented to the parish by Queen Caroline, and the Brattle Organ. Made in Oxford, England, in 1708, this is said to be the oldest working pipe organ in America. You may see a rare "vinegar" bible, so called because of a misprint — vinegar instead of vineyard — when published at Oxford in 1717. This is one of a dozen vinegar bibles in existence. Before leaving the church be sure to look at the trompe l'oeil painting on the ceiling (603-436-8232, www.stjohnsnh.org).

Continue along Chapel Street to the corner of Daniel Street. The Warner House (4), built in 1710, will be on the left at 150 Daniel Street. This brick city mansion is the finest of its kind in New England. Its interior is decorated with the oldest murals in the United States, period furnishings, and colonial-era portraits. The Warner house is open for tours (603-436-5909).

On the opposite side of Chapel Street is the old Portsmouth High School (5), constructed in 1855. It then became Portsmouth's City Hall from 1910 to 1990. Cross Daniel Street and continue to walk along Chapel Street to State Street.

Option D: Temple Israel is at 200 State Street. Built in 1827 as a Methodist Church, the local Russian Jewish community acquired the building in 1912 and adapted it for use as a temple.

Governor John Langdon House

From Chapel turn left onto State Street and walk as far as Marcy Street. Turn right onto Marcy Street. The Strawberry Banke Museum will be on the right.

Option E: Strawbery Banke Museum was founded in 1958 as "a neighborhood where the past is forever present." Ten acres have been restored in the Puddle Dock area. You may visit more than 45 buildings illustrating three-and-a-half centuries of Portsmouth history. Strawbery Banke mounts special exhibits. A shop and café are on the premises (603-433-1100, www.strawberybanke.org).

Cross Marcy Street and visit Prescott Park (6). The focal point of the park is the liberty pole. The first pole was put here in 1766 to protest the Stamp Act. Successive replicas have been erected since. The surrounding Liberty Gardens are planted and tended by the University of New Hampshire. Be sure to visit the two warehouses in the park: the 1705 Sheafe Warehouse, which has exhibits on boat-building, and the 19th-century Shaw Warehouse. The park faces the Portsmouth Naval Shipyard, which opened in 1790. The treaty ending the Russo-Japanese War was signed at the shipyard in 1905. Today it is a submarine construction and repair station.

Continue along Marcy Street and turn left onto Mechanic Street. Walk to the Point of Graves Burial Ground (7). The cemetery dates to the 1670s.

Turn right and walk to the Wentworth-Gardner House (8) at 50 Mechanic Street. This splendid block-front Georgian mansion was built in 1760 and was later acquired by New York's Metropolitan Museum of Art. A grass-roots movement in Portsmouth saved the house from being transplanted to Manhattan. Open for tours (603-436-4406; www.seacoastnh.com/wentworth).

Turn right onto Hunking Street and stop at the Tobias Lear House (9), built in 1740, at number 35. Lear was secretary to George Washington. The house is open to the public (603-436-4406; www.seacoastnh.com/lear/).

At the end of Hunking Street the Children's Museum (10) will be on the right at 280 Marcy Street. The museum is housed in an 1866 church, which was later used as a school and a town meeting place. An earlier meetinghouse (1731) stood on the site. Interactive exhibits in the museum allow children to explore and learn about nature, science, and art (603-436-3853, www.childrens-museum.org).

Walk to the back of the Children's Museum and turn right onto Manning Street. Then turn left onto Gates Street. At the end of Gates Street is Haven Park (11). The equestrian statue honors Portsmouth native and Civil War General Fitz-John Porter.

Turn right onto Pleasant Street and stop at the Governor John Langdon House and Garden (12), completed in 1785, at number 143. John Langdon had a distinguished career as a delegate to the Constitutional Convention in 1787, a U.S. Senator, and three-term New Hampshire governor. George Washington dined at the house on several occasions and admired it. A Colonial Revival dining room was added by McKim, Mead, and White in 1906. The gardens feature a pavilion, grape and rose arbors, and perennial flower beds. This is an SPNEA property, and visitors are welcomed (603-436-3205, www.spnea.org).

Continue to walk along Pleasant Street, returning to the starting point at Market Square. En route note the U.S. Custom House (13), built in 1860 of New Hampshire granite, on your left.

38 · Exeter

Directions: *By car:* Take I-95 north to exit 2, then NH 101 west to NH 108 south to Exeter. *By public transportation:* AMTRAK (1-800-USA-RAIL, www.amtrak.com) offers service to Exeter.

A group from the Massachusetts Bay Colony founded Exeter in 1638 on the shores of the Exeter and Squamscott Rivers. The town's early growth was slowed by a series of Indian attacks from 1675 to 1725. In more peaceful times Exeter became a shipbuilding center and, during the American Revolution, a provincial capital. The town's most widely known asset, Phillips Exeter Academy, was founded in 1781.

This walk begins at the American Independence Museum at One Governor's Lane (1), which provides an excellent introduction to the town's history from 1720 to 1820. The museum site has two buildings: the Ladd-Gilman House (1721) and the Folsom Tavern (c. 1775). The house tour includes displays of historic documents, portraits, military uniforms, Revolutionary War weapons, furniture, silver, and textiles. An ongoing exhibit is titled "All my Wareing apparill: Production, Consumption, and the Culture of Women's Clothing in Revolutionary Exeter." The Folsom Tavern is being restored as an education center and a place for special

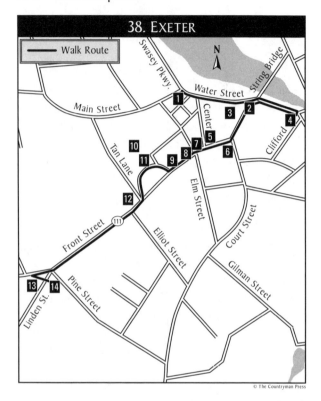

38. EXETER

Walk Route

Swasey Pkwy.

String Bridge

Water Street

Main Street

Center

Clifford

Tan Lane

Elm Street

Court Street

Front Street

Elliot Street

Gilman Street

Pine Street

Linden St.

N

© The Countryman Press

events. The house and tavern are both National Landmark Properties (603-772-2622, www.independencemuseum.org).

The museum borders Water Street. Walk along Water Street to the bandstand at the corner of Water and Front Streets. The first bandstand was placed here in 1895. It was a wooden structure and was replaced with the present Swasey Pavilion (2) in 1916. The pavilion was designed by Henry Bacon, whose best-known work is the Lincoln Memorial in Washington, D.C. The roof tiles are bronze and the interior ceiling is covered with mosaic tiles. The Exeter Brass Band, founded in 1847, gives summer concerts here.

Turn your attention to Town Hall (3). An Italianate design built in 1855, its cupola is topped with the *Statue of Justice*. The present statue was placed here in 1992, replacing the first, which had become quite weatherworn. Next door to Town Hall is the Palladian-style Congregational Church (1798).

Walk to the Gilman Garrison House (4) at 12 Water Street. Along the way you'll see the IOKA Theatre on the left, built in 1915. The epic film *Birth of the Nation* was the opening feature in this theater.

Visit the Gilman Garrison House. Garrisons (or fortifications) were commonplace in this area until the Treaty of Paris was signed in 1763 and the threat of Indian attacks was diminished. Builder John Gilman owned sawmills, and the walls of his house are constructed of huge sawn logs. His descendants later enlarged and remodeled, adding elegant paneling. A property of the Society for the Preservation of New England Antiquities, it is open to visitors (603-436-3205, www.spnea.org).

Return to Town Hall and walk along Front Street. The Methodist Church (5) on the right at 24 Front Street, originally a Unitarian church, was built in 1845. Opposite the Methodist church is the former Squamscott House (6), built in 1851, which is said to be the birthplace of the Republican Party following a meeting there in 1853. Number 41 Front Street, constructed sometime around 1780, is the Governor Jeremiah Smith House (7). A governor of New Hampshire, Smith delivered the eulogy at George Washington's funeral.

The house is on the National Register of Historic Places and is open to the public as an operating inn (603-778-7770, www.portsmouth.com./jeremiahsmithinn/).

Cross Spring Street to the Exeter Baptist Church (8). Baptists gathered in Exeter in 1800. Their first meeting-house was built in 1805, the second in 1833. The present Gothic Revival church (a Peabody and Stearns design) was constructed in 1875.

The next stop is the Exeter Historical Society (9). The society occupies a yellow brick classical revival building (1894), which for many years was the town's library. Its museum and library are open to visitors (603-778-2335, www.exeternh.org/hist/).

Continue onto the campus of Phillips Exeter Academy (603-772-4311, www.exeter.edu), which residents John and Elizabeth Phillips founded in 1781. It is a private, coeducational secondary school that attracts students from a broad spectrum of economic, racial, geographic, and religious backgrounds. The large red brick building at the head of the semicircular drive is the Fourth Academy Building (10). Designed by Ralph Adams Cram in 1914, the Georgian Revival building is similar in appearance to the second building (1794) that stood on this site. Among other things, the Academy Building houses an Anthropology Museum, which is open to the public.

As you face the Academy Building, the Frederick R. Mayer Art Center and Lamont Gallery (11) is on the left. The gallery (and the Grill adjacent to it) are open to the public (603-772-4311).

Phillips Church (12) stands at the corner of Front Street and Tan Lane. The Gothic Revival church was an early work of medievalist and architect Ralph Adams

Cram. Cram is probably best known for the nave at the Cathedral of St. John the Divine and also St. Thomas Church, both in New York City. Built as a Congregational Church in 1899, the building is now used by the academy in an interdenominational capacity.

The fork at Front and Linden Streets forms Gale Park (13). Note the World War I memorial that was modeled by one of America's best-known sculptors, Daniel Chester French, an Exeter native. He also created the seated Abraham Lincoln at the Lincoln Memorial in Washington, D.C.

To the left of the park, at One Pine Street, is the Moses-Kent House (14). Built in 1868, the house is filled with Kent family furnishings, decorative arts, and memorabilia. The landscaping is attributed to Frederick Law Olmsted. Both the house and the gardens are open to visitors (603-772-2044; www.volunteersolutions.org/uwgs/volunteer/agency/one).

39 · Concord

Directions: *By car:* Take I-93 north to exit 14. Follow the signs to the State House. *By public transportation:* Concord Trailways (1-800-639-3317, www.concordtrailway.com) and Peter Pan Bus Lines (1-800-343-9999, www.peter-panbus.com) both offer service to Concord.

Concord began in the 1660s as a trading post in the wilderness. At first a part of Massachusetts, it was first incorporated as Rumford in 1733. Three decades later the English Privy Council settled a dispute, declaring that the town was in New Hampshire. Reflecting the peaceful solution to the dispute, the town was renamed Concord in 1765 and became the state's capital in 1808. Later in the 19th century the Concord Coach was developed by two of the city's coachmakers. Manufactured by the hundreds and used by Wells Fargo and other lines, the Concord Coach played a significant role in opening the American West.

Begin at the New Hampshire State House (1). From North Main Street walk under the Memorial Arch and enter the State House Park. The arch, complete with Florentine lanterns, was placed here in 1891 under the direction of landscape architect Frederick Law Olmsted.

As you face the capitol there is a replica of the Liberty Bell on your left, a gift from the people of France.

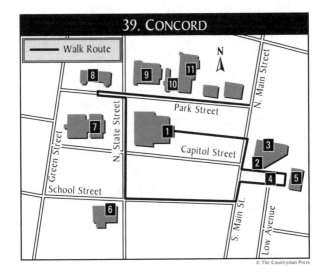

The park is dotted with monuments, including five statues of New Hampshire notables: President Franklin Pierce, statesman Daniel Webster, Revolutionary War General John Stark (who coined the state's motto: "Live free or die"), John Park Hale (U.S. Senator, ambassador, and abolitionist), and Civil War hero Commodore George Hamilton Perkins, whose statue was modeled by Daniel Chester French.

A black walnut tree, transplanted from George Washington's home at Mount Vernon, shades the northwest corner of the park.

Ground was broken for the statehouse in 1816 and it was completed in two years. The cupola, the second to crown the statehouse, was placed in 1864. It is a copy of the drum and dome atop the 17th-century Hotel des Invalides in Paris. Note the eagle perched on top of the dome. The original wooden eagle, made in 1819, was replaced with this copper copy in 1957. The old eagle is in the Tuck Library on Park Street.

Concord granite was used to build the capital. The stonecutting was done by prison inmates. Over the years the statehouse has been enlarged, doubling in size in 1864 and again in 1909. Despite expansions, this is the oldest capitol building in the United States in which the legislature uses its original chambers. Interestingly, the New Hampshire House of Representatives, with four hundred members, is the third-largest legislative body in the English-speaking world. The U.S. House and the British Parliament are larger.

Step inside the state house. The visitors center is in room 119. The capitol has over two hundred paintings, depicting more than three hundred years of New Hampshire history. Be sure to visit the Hall of Flags, Senate Chamber, Representatives Hall, Governor's Reception Room, and the Executive Council Chamber. The Office of the Secretary of State is visited by presidential hopefuls as they register for the New Hampshire primary. A gallery of photos in the office documents historic primaries (603-271-2154, www.state.nh.us).

When you leave the statehouse pass under the Memorial Arch again and return to North Main Street. Note the Concord Clock (2) across the street, which will be the next stop.

The clock was originally placed on top of the Board of Trade Building in 1872. It was restored and moved here in 1998. The steel bell weighs over 2,000 pounds and was a gift of George A. Pillsbury in 1873. The Concord Clock is maintained by the New Hampshire Historical Society.

Next to the clock is the former Eagle Hotel (3) at 110

State Capitol

North Main Street. Named for the eagle perched atop the statehouse dome, the 1851 hotel accommodated many presidents and other notables, but closed in 1961.

Walk under the arch and enter Eagle Square (4). On your right is a permanent display of capitals, finials, and other architectural detail salvaged from local buildings. The Museum of New Hampshire History (5) is operated by the New Hampshire Historical Society and is the state's only statewide history museum. Among the hundreds of pieces of art and artifacts in the collection, perhaps the most noteworthy is an authentic, well-preserved Concord Coach (603-226-3189, www.nhhistory.org).

After visiting the museum leave Eagle Square and turn left, walking south on North Main Street. Both sides of the street are lined with late-19th-century commercial buildings. Turn up School Street. The First Church of Christ Scientist (6) is at the corner of School and North State Streets. Mary Baker Eddy, the founder of the Christian Science Church, was born in Concord and lived in the city for many years. She helped finance the construction of this church. Completed in 1904, it is built of Concord granite. The 165-foot steeple is the city's tallest structure.

Walk north on North State Street toward the State House. In back of the capitol is the Legislative Office Building (7). Built in 1884 as a courthouse and post office, the New Hampshire granite building combines a number of architectural styles popular in the 19th century: High Gothic, Romanesque Revival, and French chateauesque. It was converted for use as office space in 1973.

Stand at the corner of North State and Park Streets. On the left, at 30 Park, is the New Hampshire Historical Society's Tuck Library (8). The society was founded in 1823, and the neoclassical library building was completed in 1911. Guy Lowell, who designed Boston's Museum of Fine Arts, was the library's architect. The sculpture over the door was modeled by Daniel Chester French. The exterior is Concord granite, and the interior is fitted with Italian marble. Among the artifacts is the

1819 wooden eagle that once topped the State House dome (603-225-3381, www.nhhistory.org).

Turn right onto Park Street. On the left is the New Hampshire State Library (9)—the oldest state library in the nation. Built in 1894, the Richardsonian Romanesque facade incorporates two New Hampshire granites: pink from Conway and gray from Concord.

The Upham-Walker House (10) is at 18 Park Street. Built in 1831, this Federal house was home to several generations of the same family until 1978. Today it is opened to the public for tours (603-271-2017; www. geocities.com/uphamwalkerhouse/).

Next door is St. Paul's Episcopal Church (11). The Gothic Revival church was designed by Richard Upjohn, whose most famous work is Trinity Church on Wall Street, in New York City. The church, built in 1859, suffered a devastating fire in 1984. Sadly, the interior was not restored and today incorporates modern features (603-224-2523). Continue down Park Street to North Main Street and the end of this walk.

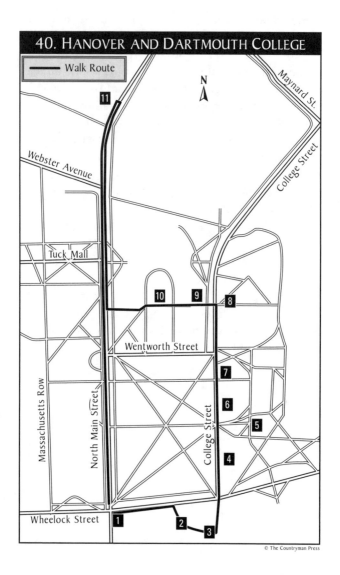

40. HANOVER AND DARTMOUTH COLLEGE

— Walk Route

N

Maynard St.

11

Webster Avenue

College Street

Tuck Mall

10 **9** **8**

Wentworth Street

Massachusetts Row

North Main Street

College Street

7

6

5

4

Wheelock Street

1 **2** **3**

© The Countryman Press

40·Hanover and Dartmouth College

Directions: Take I-93 north to I-89 north. Take exit 18 and follow NH 120 north 5 miles to Hanover. In Hanover turn left onto Wheelock Street. *By public transportation:* Dartmouth Coach (1-800-637-0123, www.concordtrailways.com/dartmouth_coach) and Vermont Transit (1-800-642-3133, www.vermonttransit.com) offer service to Hanover.

Hanover was founded by citizens of Hanover, Connecticut, who sailed up the Connecticut River and settled here in 1765. In like manner Dartmouth College has its roots in Connecticut: it began as an extension of Moor's Indian Charity School, a Connecticut mission. Named for the school's trustee, the second Earl of Dartmouth, the college began in a log cabin in the New Hampshire woods.

This tour begins at the corner of Main and Wheelock Streets just outside the door of the Hanover Inn (1). There has been an inn on this site for over 200 years. From the front door turn right onto Wheelock Street and begin to explore the college campus (603-646-1110, www.dartmouth.edu). The Hopkins Center (2) will be on the right. Built in 1962, it was designed by architect Wallace Harrison and was the prototype for one of his later works: the Metropolitan Opera House at New York's Lincoln Center. Dartmouth's main venue for the performing and creative arts, the center connects, by way of restaurants and the Hinman Post Office, to the Hood Museum of Art (3). This is one of the oldest college museums in the nation. The present building was completed in 1985 and houses a collection of 60,000 objects: American, European, African, Native American, and ancient. American artists Gilbert Stuart, Frederic Remington, and Thomas Eakins are represented, and there is an extensive collection of Old Master paintings and prints. Mexican artist José Clemente Orozco's largest mural in the United States is a part of the collection (603-646-2808, www.dartmouth.edu/~hood).

As you leave the museum the Romanesque Revival Wilson Hall (1884) will be on the right.

Cross Wheelock Street to the green. Walk up College Street. On the right is a series of halls known as Dartmouth Row. The first, built sometime around 1830, is Reed Hall (4), where in 1896 X rays were used for the first time for medical purposes in America. Next is Thornton Hall (5), completed in 1828. The larger building with a central cupola is Dartmouth Hall (6). The first Dartmouth Hall was built in 1784 and was damaged by fires in 1798, 1904, and 1935. Over the years the hall has been a dormitory, medical school, chapel, science laboratory, and a library. Today it houses lecture halls and several academic departments.

The last building on Dartmouth Row is Wentworth Hall (7). It is named for the last Royal Governor of New Hampshire, John Wentworth, who obtained a charter

Dartmouth Hall

for the college from King George III in 1769. It was built sometime around 1830, and Robert Frost lived here while a Dartmouth student.

Continue up College Street. Rollins Chapel (8) will be on the right. Named for its benefactor, Edward A.

Rollins (class of 1851), the Romanesque Revival chapel was built in the 1880s.

Webster Hall (9) is across College Street. Named for Daniel Webster, who was a New Hampshire native, Dartmouth alumnus, lawyer, congressman, senator, secretary of state, and great orator, the hall contains the college's archives.

Dominating the green is Baker Library (10), built in 1928. Enter the library and explore the Sanborn and College History Rooms on the first floor. Be sure to go to the basement and look at the murals by Mexican artist José Clemente Orozco. They were painted in 1934 and depict the artist's interpretation of the history of the Americas.

After leaving the library turn right. At North Main Street turn right again.

The Webster Cottage Museum (11) is at 32 North Main Street. This 1780 farmhouse was the home of Daniel Webster and displays many of his possessions, as well as photographs and local memorabilia. The museum is opened to the public by the Hanover Historical Society (603-643-6529).

Reverse direction and walk down North Main Street toward the Hanover Inn. The Rockefeller Center, on Webster Avenue, will be on the right. It was named for Nelson A. Rockefeller (class of 1930, three-time governor of New York, and vice president of the United States). Continue down North Main Street, past a series of early-19th-century red-brick Georgian Halls on the right. The tour ends at the Hanover Inn, where it began.

VI. Vermont

41 · Bennington

Directions: *By car:* Take I-90 (Massachusetts Turnpike) west to exit 2. Take US 20 north to US 7 north to Bennington. *By public transportation:* Bonanza Bus Lines (1-888-751-8800, www.bonanzabus.com) and Vermont Transit (1-800-642-3133, www.vermonttransit.com) offer service to Bennington.

Benning Wentworth, governor of New Hampshire, issued the grant to settle this area in 1761. The town was named Bennington in his honor. Just 16 years later the town became famous for the Battle of Bennington, on August 16, 1777, when patriot soldiers led by Gen. John Stark defeated British forces here.

This tour begins at the Bennington Battle Monument (1). The monument stands on the site of the weapons storehouse that the British hoped to capture. In 1891, during the centennial celebration of Vermont's admission to the union, the blue dolomite obelisk was dedicated. At 306 feet, it is the tallest structure in the Green Mountain State.

From April through October the monument is open to visitors. The museum at its base has a diorama of the battle, and an elevator rises to an observation room. Three states may be seen from the monument (802-447-0550; www.historicvermont.org).

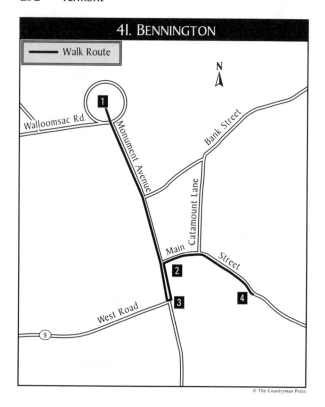

41. BENNINGTON

— Walk Route

N

Walloomsac Rd.

Monument Avenue

Bank Street

Catamount Lane

Main Street

West Road

9

© The Countryman Press

After visiting the monument walk down Monument Avenue. This was Bennington's main thoroughfare in colonial times. At the head of Monument Avenue, just in front of the obelisk, is a statue of Col. Seth Warner, a leader in the battle and a commander of Vermont's Green Mountain Boys. The granite statue was placed here in 1910.

The Federal-, Greek Revival-, and shingle-style homes that line Monument Avenue are all private residences.

The Bennington Museum

The stone house on the left was built as a blacksmith shop in 1781. Today the exterior includes 20th-century Colonial Revival details.

Beyond Bank Street note the red brick Federal-style school building on the left that was built in 1821.

Just beyond the school on the left is an 1877 statue of a catamount, or panther. It stands on the site of the old Catamount Tavern, which was destroyed by fire in 1871. The Bennington Museum, visited later on this tour, has an exhibit that recounts the tavern's story.

Bennington Center Cemetery (2) is at the foot of Monument Avenue. Established in 1762, this is the oldest cemetery in Vermont. American, British, and Hessian Revolutionary War soldiers are buried here, as are five Vermont governors. Bennington resident Robert Frost is also buried in this cemetery. His tombstone epitaph reads: "I had a lover's quarrel with the world."

Note the many 18th- and 19th-century tombstones, their inscriptions, and the stonecutters' artwork.

The Old First Church (Congregational) (3) was officially designated "Vermont's Colonial Shrine" by the state legislature. This, the first Protestant congregation in Vermont, first gathered in 1762. The present church was dedicated in 1806 and is considered one of the most beautiful churches in New England. The interior has original box pews and a plaster vaulted ceiling.

Retrace your steps to Main Street, turn right, and walk down the hill. The Bennington Museum (4) will be on the right. Best known for its extensive collection of paintings and memorabilia by local artist Grandma Moses, its Americana collection is extensive and varied: paintings, sculpture, furniture, glass, Bennington pottery, and military artifacts (802-447-1571, www.benningtonmuseum.com).

42·Woodstock

Directions: *By car:* Take I-93 north to I-89 north. Take exit 1, US 4 west, to Woodstock. *By public transportation:* Vermont Transit (1-800-642-3133, www.vermonttransit.com) offers service to Woodstock.

Woodstock enjoys a peaceful setting, buffered by the Ottauquechee River and verdant hills. A historical marker recalls the town's early history:

Woodstock
Chartered 1761. Settled 1768. Famous for the architecture of its houses and churches, Woodstock is the only town in America with four Paul Revere church bells.

The Windsor county seat since colonial times, Woodstock has long been home to lawyers, doctors, teachers, merchants, and other professionals who, in the 18th and 19th centuries, lined the town's streets with fine houses, churches, and public buildings, most of which have been well preserved. An interesting aside: the country's first ski tow was operated at Mount Tom in Woodstock in 1934.

Begin the walking tour of historic Woodstock at the town green. The Norman Williams Public Library (1) is a Romanesque Revival building. The gift of Dr.

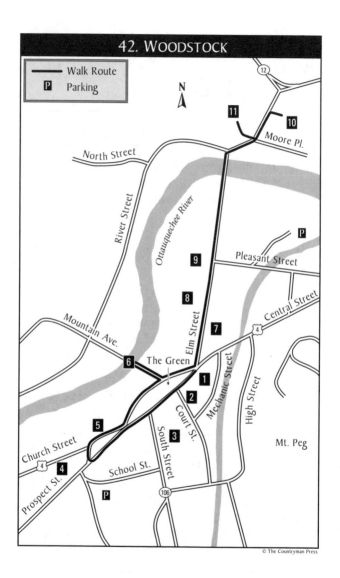

42. WOODSTOCK

- —— Walk Route
- **P** Parking

N

12

11   **10**
Moore Pl.

North Street

River Street

Ottauquechee River

P
Pleasant Street

9

Central Street

8

Mountain Ave.

Elm Street

7

4

Mechanic Street

6   The Green

1

High Street

2

Mt. Peg

5

Court St.

3

South Street

Church Street

4

School St.

Prospect St.

P

106

© The Countryman Press

Edward H. Williams in 1883, the library includes a collection of books about local history.

Make your way around the green in a clockwise direction. Next to the library is the cupola-topped Windsor County Courthouse (2). The Woodstock Inn (3) is next door. In the 18th century the Eagle Tavern stood on this site. It was replaced by the Woodstock Inn in 1893, which has since been expanded and updated. As you continue to circle around the green, three early 19th-century houses are just beyond the inn. The original jail, which dates to 1786, is followed by the 1807 headquarters of the Daughters if the American Revolution. St. James Episcopal Church (4), completed in 1907, faces the green. The bell in its tower is one of the four Paul Revere bells in Woodstock.

Turn to face the green. Town Hall (5), built in 1899, is on the left. Between Town Hall and the covered bridge is a row of houses built between 1803 and 1823. Walk over the Middle Covered Bridge (6), and then return to the green again. Note the Federal-period houses on the left as you approach Elm Street. At Elm and Center Streets you'll see the Cabot Block (7) across the way. Turn left onto Elm Street. The Dana House Museum (8) will be on the left at number 26. Run by the Woodstock Historical Society, the museum exhibits its exceptional collection of paintings, toys, furniture, historic costumes, textiles, and other artifacts that illustrate Woodstock's history (802-457-1822; www.woodstockhistoricalsoc.org). The First Congregation Church (9), built in 1808, is the white, Greek Revival church. It, too, houses a Paul Revere bell. Across Elm Street is another row of houses dating from the 1820s.

Cross the Ottauquechee River on the trestle bridge.

Billings Farm and Museum

Continue on to two more sites: the Billings Farm and Museum (10) on your right and the Marsh-Billings-Rockefeller National Historic Park (11) on your left. A good place to begin a visit is at the farm's visitor center, where an excellent orientation film is shown. Continue your visit in the 1890 Farmhouse. The museum is housed in a series of 19th-century barns, and period farm life is illustrated through a series of exhibits. The farm was established in 1871; Frederick Billings imported his dairy herd from the Isle of Jersey. Jersey cows and other livestock may been seen on this, an operating farm (802-457-2355, www.billingsfarm.org).

The Marsh-Billings-Rockefeller National Historic Park is across the road from the Billings Farm. The Queen Anne–style mansion houses an impressive collection of 19th-century American paintings, including works by Thomas Cole, John Kensett, and Albert Bierstadt. Furniture and porcelain are also on display. The park service's visitors center is in the Carriage Barn (802-457-3368, www.nps.gov.mabi). Be sure to visit the gardens, forest trails, and carriage roads in this 550-acre park. The trails that climb Mount Tom feature several overlooks offering splendid panoramic views at the end of this walk.

VII. Maine

43 · York Village

Directions: *By car:* Take I-95 north to exit 4, signed The Yorks. Take US 1 south for ¼ mile to the traffic light. Turn left onto York Street, US 1A, and follow it to York Village. There is no public transportation to York Village.

Captain John Smith explored this area in 1614, and called it Agamenticus. In 1641 it became the first English city chartered in the Americas. No longer a city, the town of York, named for York, England, is known for its colonial sites, beaches, and picturesque harbors.

The tour begins at Jefferd's Tavern (1). Seven of the historic buildings on this walk are maintained and opened by the Old York Historical Society (207-363-4974, www.oldyork.org). Tickets to the society's buildings are on sale at the tavern. The tavern was built in the neighboring town of Wells in 1750. Restored in the 1940s, it was moved here in 1959. The interior features a beehive brick oven, murals by the 19th century itinerant artist Rufus Porter, and a taproom with a bar cage.

The Old School House (2), built in 1745, is next to the tavern. Walk down Lindsay Road for about ½ mile. The John Hancock Warehouse (3), which dates to the 1740s, is set on the banks of the York River. In colonial times the river served York as a highway would today, and this is the sole remaining warehouse of the many

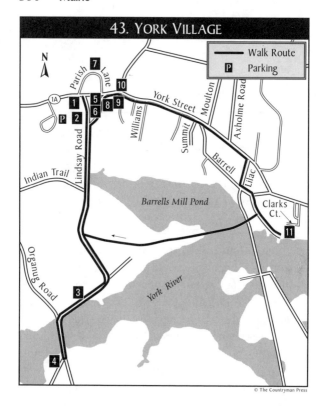

43. YORK VILLAGE

— Walk Route

P Parking

N

Parish Lane

1A

York Street

Williams

Lindsay Road

Indian Trail

Organug Road

Barrells Mill Pond

Moulton

Summit

Barrell

Axholme Road

Lilac

Clarks Ct.

York River

© The Countryman Press

that once dotted the riverfront. Owned by John Hancock, who had family in York, the warehouse was bought by George Marshall in 1867. Marshall built the store next door. The George Marshall store today has gallery space where changing exhibits are mounted.

After seeing the warehouse and store continue to walk along Lindsay Road. Turn left onto Organug Road and cross the York River on the 18th-century Sewall's Bridge. The Elizabeth Perkins House (4) will be on the right. The oldest part of the house dates to 1686; additions were made in 1730 and again in the early 20th century. This is an excellent example of an early 20th-century Colonial Revival house, its large, comfortable rooms furnished with 18th-century furniture and decorative arts.

After the Elizabeth Perkins House retrace your steps on Lindsay Road to the corner of York Street and the 17th-century Burying Ground (5). The Emerson-Wilcox House (6) abuts the Burying Ground. Built in 1742 and enlarged in 1760 and again in 1817, this has been a home, a stagecoach stop, a tavern, a general store, and a tailor's shop. Today the museum houses 12 period rooms and two galleries exhibiting furniture, silver, textiles, and ceramics. Across York Street is the First Parish Church (7), built in 1747. Note the steeple, based on those designed by Sir Christopher Wren. John Hancock's grandfather was the minister here from 1690 to 1698.

Farther along York Street is the Old Gaol (8). Built in 1719, the Old Gaol includes timbers used in the previous prison, built in 1656. Not only does the gaol have prisoners' dungeons and cells, but living quarters for the jailer and his family. Of special note: candlelight tours and theatrical living history presentations are given by actors on Friday and Saturday evenings. Contact the Old York Historical Society for details.

The Society's administrative offices and research library are at 207 York Street (9), and the museum shop is just across the street.

Note the Soldiers and Sailors Monument (10) in the middle of the intersection. The statue was chiseled from a single piece of granite by artist Frederick Bancroft in 1906. Some feel that the statue is a curiosity, because it

OLD YORK HISTORICAL SOCIETY

The Old Gaol

is a Civil War monument yet the soldier is wearing the
uniform used by the army some years later during the
Spanish American War.

Continue on York Street and turn right onto Lilac
Lane. Then turn left onto Barrell Lane and left again
onto Barrell Lane Extension. You have arrived at the
Sayward-Wheeler House (11), built in 1713. Jonathan
Sayward was a wealthy merchant and a judge. A prop-
erty of the Society for the Preservation of New England
Antiquities, the house is open for tours (603-436-3205,
www.spnea.org).

After seeing the Sayward-Wheeler House follow the
river toward the ocean along the Fisherman's Path. To
return to town, cross Lilac Road at the Sayward-Wheeler
House, and take the path to the Wiggley Bridge. Cross
the bridge and continue on the path to Lindsay Road
where the tour began.

44·Kennebunkport

Directions: *By car:* Take I-95 north to exit 3, signed for Kennebunk. Follow ME 35 east to Kennebunkport. *By public transportation:* Take AMTRAK (1-800-USA-RAIL, www.amtrak.com) to Wells, Maine. From Wells take a Front Line Taxi (1-866-490-1214) for the 10-minute ride to Kennebunkport.

The name Kennebunkport is derived from the Indian word meaning "long sandbar." The town, first settled in 1639, is picturesquely situated where the Kennebunk River meets the Atlantic Ocean. A thriving shipbuilding center in the 1700s, Kennebunkport and Cape Arundel have long since become a haven for artists, literati, and summer residents.

This is one of the longer walks in this guide. The first half, about 3 miles, focuses on historic sites in town. The second half, about 2 miles, follows the coast. Allow a full day for the entire tour.

Begin at Dock Square (1). The monument in Dock Square "dedicated to Our Soldiers and Sailors" was erected in 1909. As you look back toward the Kennebunk River, the old Rum Warehouse (1775) is just to the left of ME 9. In colonial times ships voyaged between here and the West Indies, trading Maine lumber for West Indian molasses, used in distilling rum.

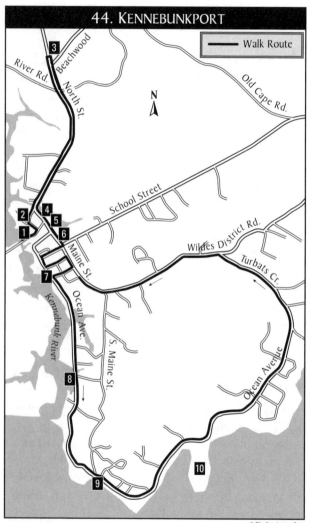

44. KENNEBUNKPORT

Walk Route

River Rd.
Beachwood
North St.
Old Cape Rd.

N

School Street

Wildes District Rd.

Turbats Cr.

Maine St.

Ocean Ave.

Kennebunk River

S. Maine St.

Ocean Avenue

1 2 3 4 5 6 7 8 9 10

© The Countryman Press

Walk along Spring Street and turn left onto Temple Street. The South Congregational Church (2), built in 1824, stands at the end of Temple. The steeple was inspired by churches in London designed by Sir Christopher Wren. The columned portico was added in 1912. After seeing the church and the church green turn left onto North Street. Walk north about a mile to the History Center of Kennebunkport (3). The center has four buildings clustered on the same site: the Town House School, the Old Jail Cells, the Clark Shipwright's Office, and the Pasco Exhibit Center (297-967-2751, www.kporthistory.org).

Retrace your steps from the History Center to the village. When you reach Temple Street and the river, bear left onto Maine Street. On the left is the Village Baptist Church (4), completed in 1838. Though a Federal-style church, it may also be labeled a transitional church, in that it does incorporate some early Gothic Revival detailing. Just beyond the church, to the left, is the Greek Revival Nott House (5), built in 1853. The house is filled with furnishings collected by four generations of the Perkins and Nott families. Bequeathed to the historical society in 1981, the Nott House is open for tours (201-967-2751, www.kporthistory.org).

Continue along Maine Street to Mast Cove Lane. The Louis T. Graves Memorial Library (6) will be on the left. Built in 1813 as a bank building, it became the U.S. Custom House in 1831, a library in 1898, and is now a memorial to the son of local artist Abbott Graves.

Kennebunkport is a textbook of 18th- and 19th-century architecture. The Colonial, Federal, and Victorian periods are all represented among the well-preserved houses lining the village's tree shaded streets. For an overview, turn left onto Maine Street after leaving the library. Then turn right onto Elm Street. At the end of Elm Street turn left onto Ocean Avenue and left again onto Pearl Street. At the end of Pearl Street turn right onto Maine Street and then right again onto Green Street.

The Arundel Yacht Club (7) is at the intersection of Green Street and Ocean Avenue. The clubhouse dates to 1806 and was originally part of a ropewalk, a long building where ropes are manufactured. From Green Street turn left onto Ocean Avenue and walk south to the Kennebunkport Maritime Heritage Association (8). Housed in the boathouse that belonged to author Booth Tarkington, the museum has a collection of ship models, maritime paintings, and artifacts. Tarkington's schooner *Regina* is also on display (207-967-8809).

This is where the first part of the Kennebunkport tour ends. It has taken you through town and its historic sites. The rest of the walk (about 2 miles) will take you along the oceanfront, through fields, and back to town.

Continue along Ocean Avenue and around Cape Arundel. The Kennebunk River is on the right and leads to the Atlantic Ocean. St. Anne's Episcopal Church (9) will be on the right. The church was built with stones gathered by parishioners. The roof is is supported by massive pine beams. Undoubtedly St. Anne's best known parishioners are former President and Mrs. George Herbert Walker Bush, whose summer home is a short distance farther on.

From Ocean Avenue two natural phenomena can be seen: Spouting Rock and Blowing Cave. Beyond these is Walker's Point (10). The stone house on the point is a former summer White House, and has been in President Bush's family for generations. Though the Secret Service prevents uninvited guests from venturing out onto the peninsula, there are excellent views from Ocean Avenue. Walk past Turbat's Creek and turn left onto Wildes District Road. This will lead back to the village.

Option A: To visit St. Anthony's Monastery and Shrine, from Dock Square walk over the bridge (ME 9) spanning the Kennebunk River. Turn left at the first corner and the Shrine will be on your left (207-967-2011).

45 • Portland

Directions: *By car:* Take I-95 north, and exit 6A to I-295 east. Take exit 4 and follow US 1 east to 1A (Commercial Street). Turn left onto High Street to the Victoria Mansion on the left at Danforth Street. *By public transportation:* Take AMTRAK (1-800-USA-Rail, www.amtrak.com), Concord Trailways (1-800-639-3317, www.concordtrailways.com), and Vermont Transit (1-800-642-3133, www.vermonttransit.com) offer service to Portland.

English settlers founded Portland in 1632. The town was given several names before it finally took that of the Isle of Portland, in Devonshire, England, in 1786. When Maine separated from Massachusetts in 1820, Portland became its capital and remained so until 1832. A fire devastated the city on July 4, 1866, but it rebuilt and grew. In addition to fishing and shipping, Portland became a major shipbuilding center during both World Wars. Beautifully sited on two peninsulas, Portland overlooks Casco Bay and its islands. Its 19th-century architecture preserved, Portland today is enjoying a resurgence and renewal.

This tour begins at the Victoria Mansion (1) at 109 Danforth Street, between Park and High Streets. The house is not named for the owner or the architect, but

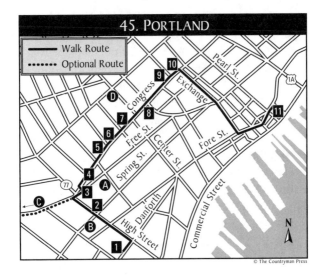

45. PORTLAND

—— Walk Route
······ Optional Route

rather for the British queen. Built between 1858 and 1860 for the New Orleans hotelier Ruggles Sylvester Morse, it was later occupied by the Libby family. The exterior of this Italianate villa is brownstone. The lavish interior is decorated with the very best money could buy: furniture, paintings, carved woodwork, stained glass, Italian marble fireplaces, and frescoes, some done in trompe l'oeil—three-dimensional scenes painted on flat walls. The result is the most sumptuous Victorian house north of Newport. The building is on the National Register of Historic Places and is open for tours (207-772-4841, www.victoria-mansion.org).

After leaving Victoria House go to High Street and walk up the hill. At the corner of High and Spring Streets, the Hugh McLellan House (2) is on the right. It was designed by Alexander Parris and built in 1800.

Note the original hand-carved fence. The McLellan House is a part of the Portland Museum of Art.

Continue up High Street. The Cumberland Club will be on the left. At Free Street turn right to the main entrance of the Portland Museum of Art (3). The museum was begun in 1882. At first housed in the McLellan House, it expanded to the beaux-arts Lorenzo de Medici Sweat Memorial Galleries in 1911. The Charles Shipman Payson Building was added in 1981, using the design of Henry Nichols Cobb of I. M. Pei and Partners. The museum's collection has over 15,000 fine and decorative arts, European and American, from the 18th century to the present. Works by Winslow Homer, Rodin, Degas, Monet, Picasso, Hassam, Lane, N. C. Wyeth, Sargent, Prendergast, Cezanne, Chagall, Daumier, and many others are on display (207-775-6148, www.portlandmuseum.org).

Option A: The Children's Museum of Maine is next door to the Portland Museum of Art at 142 Free Street. It features dozens of interactive exhibits (207-828-1234, www.kitetails.com).

Option B: The Museum of African Tribal Art is located at 122 Spring Street. African masks and other artwork are on exhibit (207-871-7188, www.africantribalartmuseum.org).

Option C: The Neal Dow Memorial is at 714 Congress Street. An abolitionist, politician, and prohibitionist, Neal Dow bequeathed his 1829 Federal house to the Maine Women's Christian Temperance Union. The house and museum are open to visitors (207-773-7773).

Resume your walk at the corner of High and Congress Streets. The Federal-style, triangular "flatiron" building (4) at the intersection of High, Free, and Congress Streets was built in 1826.

Turn right onto Congress Street. Note the large red brick building ahead on the left. The John Bundy Brown Memorial Block (5), at 529–543 Congress Street, was built in 1882. The style is Queen Anne and its facade includes red brick, terra-cotta, and freestone.

Stop at Mechanics Hall at 519 Congress Street (6). This Italianate building was constructed in 1857 and designed by Thomas J. Sparrow, a Portland native.

On the opposite side of the street, at number 522, is the Institute of Contemporary Art, a gallery managed by the Maine College of Art. The galleries are opened to the public free of charge (207-879-5742, ext. 229; www.meca.edu).

Just ahead on the left, at 485–489 Congress Street, is a one-acre site belonging to the Maine Historical Society (7), which includes the Wadsworth-Longfellow House. Built in 1785, this is the oldest house in Portland and was the childhood home of Henry Wadsworth Longfellow. The museum at the Center for Maine History and the Maine Historical Society Library are also part of the site. All three facilities are open to visitors (207-774-1822, www.mainehistory.org).

Option D: The Portland Public Market is one block north, at the corner of Preble Street and Cumberland Avenue. The award-winning timber and granite building has a wide variety of eateries, cafés, and vendors.

Continue east on Congress Street; Monument Square (8) will be on the right. The statue of *Our Lady of Victories* is the city's Civil War monument. The relief sculptures feature two Maine men: Brig. Gen. Francis L. Vinton and Adm. David G. Farragut. Maine native Franklin

McLellan House

© CRAIG BECKER, PORTLAND MUSEUM OF ART

Simmons modeled the statue while living in Italy. The 45-foot-high bronze and granite memorial was dedicated in 1888.

The First Parish Church (9) is a little farther along Congress Street on the left. It is the second church building to stand on this site. The first was built in 1749 and was affectionately known as Old Jerusalem. The present church was built in 1825 and topped with Old

Jerusalem's weathervane. The building material used was granite from Freeport, Maine (207-773-5747, www.firstparishportland.org).

Just beyond the church is City Hall (10). The first two city halls that stood on this site burned, one during the great fire of July 4, 1866, and the second in a 1908 blaze. This granite, Renaissance Revival building was designed in 1909 by Carrére and Hastings of New York City. Their most famous work is the New York Public Library.

Look straight down Congress Street to the tower in the distance. That is the Portland Observatory (1807). The 86-foot tower offers visitors not only unrivaled views of the city, the bay, and the mountains beyond, but also tours, exhibits, and a shop (207-774-5561, www.portlandmarks.org).

Walk down Exchange Street en route to the Old Port Exchange. On the left, at numbers 103–107 and 81–89, is an Italianate block built in 1866. Between them, at numbers 93–95, is the mansard-roofed Centennial Block (1876). Look ahead to the right. The trompe l'oeil mural at Tommy's Park on Middle Street was painted in 1985 by Portland artists Michael Lewis and Chris Denison.

On the left at 56 Exchange Street is the Queen Anne–style First National Bank Block (1883). The facade includes brick, sandstone, and terra-cotta. Walk to Fore Street. At 384–392 Fore Street is an 1854 Greek Revival block that survived the 1866 fire. Numbers 373–375 house the Seaman's Club, an 1866 Gothic Revival design. Opposite, at 366–376, is the Mariner's Church (1828). The church has both Greek Revival and Federal details. The Samuel Butts House and Store is located at 332–334 Fore Street. Built in 1792, it is one of the oldest structures in the city today.

The tour ends at the Custom House (11), built between 1868 and 1871. Both exterior and interior of this granite, mansard-style building are remarkably well preserved.

Index